Gifted Children and Legal Issues:
An Update

Frances A. Karnes
and
Ronald G. Marquardt

Gifted Psychology Press, Inc.

Gifted Children and Legal Issues: An Update

Cover Design: Stephanie Polhamus
Interior Design: Spring Winnette
Indexer: Spring Winnette

Published by
Gifted Psychology Press, Inc.
P.O. Box 5057
Scottsdale AZ 85261

© 2000 by Gifted Psychology Press, Inc.
Printed and bound in the United States of America

05 04 03 02 01 00   6 5 4 3 2 1

Library of Congress Cataloging-in-Publication Data

Karnes, Frances A.
  Gifted children and legal issues : an update / Frances A. Karnes and Ronald G. Marquardt.
    p. cm.
  Includes bibliographical references and index.
  ISBN 0-910707-34-0
  1. Gifted children–Education–Law and legislation–United States. 2. Gifted children–Legal status, laws, etc.–United States. I. Marquardt, Ronald G., 1939- II. Title.

KF4209.5 .K369 2000
344.73'07915–dc21   99-047765

ISBN 0-910707-34-0

Table of Contents

Preface v
Acknowledgments vii
Foreword by Dr. James J. Gallagher ix
Chapter 1–Federal and State Initiatives 1
Chapter 2–The Legal Process and Gifted Education 13
Chapter 3–Court Cases and Gifted Students' 19
             Educational Opportunities
Chapter 4–A Case-by-Case Look at School Policies 45
             Affecting Gifted Education
Chapter 5–Negotiation in Gifted Education 59
Chapter 6–Gifted Education and Mediation 63
Chapter 7–Gifted Education and Due Process................... 71
Chapter 8–Other Legal Issues Related to Gifted Youth 83
Chapter 9–Gifted Children and the Office for Civil 109
             Rights
Chapter 10–Gifted Legal Issues in the New Millenium.... 121
Appendix A–Jacob Javits Gifted and Talented 129
             Students Education Act of 1988
Appendix B–Table Of Cases... 139
Appendix C–State Offices of Gifted Education 143

Appendix D–State Associations for the Gifted 157

Appendix E–National Associations and Resources for 167
the Gifted

Appendix F–Position Statements of the National 171
Association for Gifted Children

About the Authors...209

Index 213

Preface

Our first two books on legal issues in gifted education, *Gifted Children and the Law: Mediation, Due Process, and Court Cases* and *Gifted Children and Legal Issues: Parents' Stories of Hope*, both published in 1991, were received enthusiastically. The continuing interest has been an incentive to keep professionals—both in the field of gifted education and those working within the legal arena—abreast of the most recent information on mediation, due process, and court cases pertaining to gifted children. Toward that end, we established The Institute for Law and Gifted Education in 1992 as part of The Center for Gifted Studies at The University of Southern Mississippi, and this Institute has become a focal point throughout the nation for information on case law and statutory law regarding gifted children.

The contents of the present book take the reader from the 1991 publications to the present. It was not our intention to rewrite these previous books, but to build upon them. We have attempted to set forth in a clear and concise manner new insights in legal issues involving gifted education. Additionally, a major new chapter not contained in the earlier books has been added to the present book. The work of the Office for Civil Rights (OCR) on behalf of gifted children is also a valuable addition.

As with the previous books, the new information in the present book is not just for school personnel, administrators, and school board members, but also for family members of gifted children. We hope that this book, and its predecessors, will also be of interest to state and national legislators, to local, state and federal directors of gifted education and related areas, and to other concerned citizens.

Acknowledgments

Many people have supported our endeavors in investigating the gifted and legal issues, and to them we express our deepest appreciation. A special note of thanks is extended to the state consultants in gifted education who continue to provide us up-to-date information on mediation, due process, and court cases. The Office for Civil Rights and the regional office personnel were prompt and thorough in forwarding of the letters of findings focusing on gifted children and youth. We are most appreciative.

The support staff at The Center for Gifted Studies who assisted in the manuscript preparation and office management are to be commended. A special thanks is extended to Heather Ratliff for her technical assistance and to Barbara Van Duser for her management skills. The insights of Kristen Stephens continue to be valuable. Our publisher, Gifted Psychology Press, Inc., offered many ideas and great skill in the editing of the manuscript. We appreciate the support of Gifted Psychology Press in producing this third volume on gifted education and legal issues.

We will always be indebted to our families who continue to encourage our academic pursuits on this important topic. To Susan, Mark, and Rick Marquardt and to Ray, John, Leighanne, and Mary Ryan Karnes, we appreciate your continued support. To Christopher Karnes, your influence will always be felt in our lives.

Foreword

In this text, Frances Karnes and Ronald Marquardt continue their significant contributions in their earlier work, *Gifted Children and the Law: Mediation, Due Process and Court Cases*. To many people in gifted education the law has played a small and insignificant role in the education of these special children.

However, appearances can be deceiving. In this volume, and in the previous ones on the same topic, there has been extensive legal action to reach accommodation between school system, and gifted children and their parents. This misperception of little action results, as the authors point out, because most of the cases involving gifted students are brought in state courts and do not have the public attention that is sometimes given cases before federal courts, or the Supreme Court.

Nor is it true, as this volume clearly points out, that the only redress that parents have is to go to the courts. There are numerous steps through due process procedures and through mediation that the parents can get issues resolved without the time consuming and costly use of the court system. The authors stress that, if at all possible, parents should try to settle their differences with the education establishment through mediation or negotiation.

The results of the many actions described here are mixed, sometimes deciding for the gifted student and sometimes for the educational establishment. There is no long history supporting parental concerns as one finds with children with disabilities where the public and legal sympathies lean in the direction of the family. Nevertheless, it is important that parents know that these options are available to them and that they are not at the mercy of unknowledgeable personnel or institutions.

I find the discussion of mediation a particularly compelling one. In a four-year period of time, the number of states offering formal mediation increased from 10 to 21, indicating the growing popularity of these processes. The authors point out that there are numerous documents and materials that states provide that can help parents prepare for such mediation.

One of the events most feared by school systems is that they will be hauled into court under charges of discriminating against bright minority students in their service provisions for gifted students. Not only do such charges result in massive loss of time and resources on the part of the school to defend against the charges, but the charges themselves are damaging to the self concept of schools that are trying to be fair and equitable to all of their students.

In this regard, there is a useful chapter on the Office for Civil Rights and the positive steps that school personnel can take to prepare for interactions with the OCR. It would help the schools to know that the majority of "findings" of OCR turn out to be in favor of the schools when they have well documented procedures for establishing eligibility for services.

Our legal system is always a court of last resort. Karnes and Marquardt have provided much usable information and advice that can make exploration of legal alternatives more thoughtful and knowledgeable. I hope they will continue to amass this library of legal information, which is valuable to those working with gifted students and for the parents of gifted students.

James J. Gallagher, Ph D.
Kenan Professor of Education
The University of North Carolina at Chapel Hill

1

Federal and State Initiatives

Federal Definitions

As we noted in 1991 in *Gifted Children and the Law*, the Federal government historically has been reluctant to become involved in educational issues, and even less involved with gifted education. Legislation introduced in the U.S. Senate (S. 505) and U.S. House of Representatives (H.R. 637) in 1999 documented the lack of federal support for gifted children. Both bills noted that for every $100 of federal funds spent on education, less than $.02 was spent on gifted education.

Although the federal government did re-establish an Office of Gifted and Talented in Washington, DC in 1988 and has funded a consortium of universities in conjunction with the National Research Center for the Gifted and Talented, the primary initiative of the Federal government has been in providing definitions of gifted and talented children and in establishing a few model programs. The Federal definitions, as we shall see later, have subsequently been used by many states.

The federal definition of gifted and talented students has evolved through several changes since first appearing in the Education Amendments of 1969 (U.S. Congress, 1970). That 1969 definition is stated as follows:

> *The term 'gifted and talented children' means in accordance with objective criteria prescribed by the Commissioner, children who have outstanding intellectual ability or creative talent, the development of which requires special activities or services not ordinarily provided by local educational agencies.*

Dr. Sidney P. Marland, the Commissioner of Education, in the 1972 report to Congress (U.S. Congress, 1970) provided another definition:

> *Gifted and talented children are those identified by professionally qualified persons who by virtue of outstanding abilities are capable of high performance. These are children who require differentiated educational programs and/or services beyond those normally provided by the regular school program in order to realize their contributions to self and society.*
>
> *Children capable of high performance include those with demonstrated and/or potential ability in any of the following areas, singly or in combination: general intellectual ability, specific academic aptitude, creative or productive thinking, leadership, visual and performing arts, and psychomotor ability.*

The above definition was modified in 1978 as follows:

> *... the term 'gifted and talented children' means children and, whenever applicable, youth, who are identified at the preschool, elementary, or secondary level as possessing demonstrated or potential abilities that give evidence of high performance capability in areas such as intellectual, creative, specific academic or leadership ability*

or in the performing and visual arts and who by reason thereof require services or activities not ordinary provided by the school.

The Jacob K. Javits Gifted and Talented Students Education Act of 1988 (U.S. Congress, 1988) modified the federal definition again to read:

The term 'gifted and talented' student means children and youth who give evidence of high performance capability in areas such as intellectual, creative, artistic or leadership capacity, or in specific fields, and who require special services or activities not ordinarily provided by the school in order to fully develop such capabilities.

In 1993, The U.S. Department of Education released its report entitled *A Case for Developing America's Talent*. The definition of gifted and talented children given in that document was:

Children and youth with outstanding talent (who) perform or show the potential for performing at remarkably high levels of accomplishment when compared with others of their age, experience, or environment.

The children and youth (who) exhibit high performance capability in intellectual, creative, and/or artistic areas, possess an unusual leadership capacity, or excel in specific academic fields. They require services or activities not ordinarily provided by the schools.

Outstanding talents are present in children and youth from all cultural groups, across all economic strata, and in all areas of human endeavor.

Despite slight wording differences, the Federal statutes have been quite consistent in their various definitions over the last three decades of the 20th century. All of the definitions note that gifted children need educational programs and/or services beyond the ordinary school curriculum. The burden has been left to individual states and municipalities to provide the additional services.

State Initiatives

Federal statutes and regulations pertaining to gifted education relate to developments at state and local levels. Of more immediate concern to parents, educators, and other advocates, however, are the relevant state and local law and policies, regulations, and guidelines. Those who urge that more be done in local schools to meet the unique needs of gifted children quickly learn that they must become very informed about the laws and regulations in their respective states. Advocates for gifted education often suspect or conclude that the laws and regulations are not stimulating and supporting adequate specialized educational opportunities for gifted children. Sometimes the laws and regulations are ignored by administrators; other times they are used to set limits on what can be undertaken to meet the special needs of gifted children. Minimum requirements, unfortunately, tend to become maximum expectations in many local schools.

Overview of State Legislation and Other Initiatives

Since state laws vary widely and are frequently revised, it is not feasible to present detailed information for all the states. Instead, we will present an overview of legislative provisions and policies that have occurred throughout the country at the end of this century. We hope this information will enable advocates for gifted education in any given state to review developments in that state and its schools in the context of what has happened elsewhere. In addition to state laws, advocates will want to become familiar with policy statements and guidelines concerning gifted education issued by state departments of education or local boards of education. These documents usually include definitions being used, criteria for selection into programs for gifted students, and the basis for state and local funding for gifted programs.

In the 1996 *State of the States Gifted and Talented Education Report*, forty-eight states completed the survey. Of those responding, 48 percent reported that their state mandated both identification and special programming for gifted children. Seventeen percent stated that there was a mandate for identification, but not for programming, and four percent reported a mandate for programming but not for identification.

Not all of the mandates were by law, however. Of those having mandates, only 58 percent were by state law. Six percent were by administrative rule, three percent by the state department of education guidelines, eighteen percent through a combination, and fifteen percent through other provisions such as policies issued by state boards of education.

Funding specifically designated for gifted child education appears to have increased somewhat in recent years. Seventy-one percent of those responding reported that states specifically allocated funds for gifted education. Fifty-five percent stated an increase in funding in the past few years, nineteen percent indicated a decrease, and 26 percent showed no change.

Administratively, gifted education efforts at the state level typically are combined with other educational efforts. Approximately two-thirds of the state consultants indicated that gifted education is under special education or curriculum and instruction in the state educational agency (SEA). Ninety-four percent reported that one or more persons were specifically designated in the SEA to have primary responsibilities to coordinate gifted education efforts in their state.

Definitions of gifted education, though varying in specific language from state to state, were typically uniform within a given state. Ninety-two percent of the states indicated that they had a specific definition, and sixty-three percent required all districts in their states to use that definition. Additionally, forty-eight percent of the states required local districts to follow a uniform process in identifying gifted children within their districts.

Stephens and Karnes (in press) surveyed state consultants in gifted education regarding state definitions of gifted and talented. Five states did not have a state-wide definition (Massachusetts, Minnesota, New Hampshire, New Jersey and South Dakota), although three of these states allowed local definitions. Twenty-one states had revised their definitions since 1990. The majority of states used some form of the 1978 federal definition. Colorado, Delaware, and Hawaii employed a form of the 1972 Marland definition.

The 1988 Javits definition is used only in Wisconsin. Intellectual aspects of giftedness were emphasized in most state definitions which included specific mention of superior intellect in their definition. Specific academic ability was mentioned in thirty-three states, creative ability in thirty, visual and performing arts in twenty, leadership in eighteen, and psychomotor in three. Almost all the states' definitions use the terms "demonstrated and/or potential achievement." Arkansas is the only state using the definition offered by Renzulli (1978). His definition of giftedness emphasizes three specific traits—above average ability, creativity, and task commitment.

Few states appear to have considered identification or services to pre-school gifted children. Only Indiana, Oklahoma, Vermont, Wyoming, and Colorado specifically mention pre-school age students in their legislative provisions or policies.

Karnes, Stephens, and Whorton (in press) surveyed state consultants to ascertain which states required teachers to have specific certification/endorsement in order to teach gifted students in specialized programs. Twenty-eight states have certification/endorsement, with three having it on an optional basis. Two require a Master's degree, and the other states have a range of six to twenty-one course hour requirements. West Virginia is the only state requiring a specific exam for certification. Eight states reported having printed standards describing competencies for teachers of the gifted in specialized programs.

Without the legal support of a federal law to mandate education for the gifted and talented, advocates for these students must rely on state law, rules and regulations, and policies and procedures. Admittedly, states have embraced mandated services somewhat more readily in the last decade of the twentieth century than at any other time in history. However, to obtain and preserve appropriate public education for all gifted and talented children and youth, rigorous attention must be maintained toward legislative mandates both at the state and national levels.

The National Association for Gifted Children has issued a position paper on mandated services for gifted children. Although not legally binding, this position paper gives support to those who advocate that schools should be required to provide differentiated educational experiences.

Position Paper

Mandated Educational Opportunities for Gifted and Talented Students

The National Association for Gifted Children (NAGC) periodically issues policy statements that deal with issues, policies, and practices that have an impact on the education of gifted and talented students. Policy statements represent the official convictions of the organization.

All policy statements approved by the NAGC Board of Directors are consistent with the organization's belief that education in a democracy must respect the uniqueness of all individuals, the broad range of cultural diversity present in our society, and the similarities and differences in learning characteristics that can be found within any group of students. NAGC is fully committed to national goals that advocate both excellence and equity for all students, and we believe that the best way to achieve these goals is through differentiated educational opportunities, resources, and encouragement for all students.

The National Association for Gifted Children supports mandating services to meet the unique needs of gifted and talented children.

Numerous studies, including the federal report National Excellence: A Case for Developing America's Talent, released in November 1993, have documented that needs of our nation's gifted and talented students are not being met. Programs for these students are currently often viewed as extracurricular and are available only on limited basis in some school systems, money permitting. The needs of gifted and talented students have been well documented by research and federal studies.

To educate all our children and allow America to compete in a global economy and all fields of human endeavor, the nation must provide an environment in which gifted and talented students, along with all of our children, can reach their full potential.

National Association for Gifted Children, 1707 L Street, Suite 550 Washington, DC 20036

In the absence of federal legislation, the policies and procedures vary dramatically from state to state. Clearly, it is essential that advocates in a given state become informed directly regarding current laws, and relevant state and local policy and guideline documents. Needless to say, one must not rely on hearsay or on information from casual conversations when preparing to represent the interests of gifted children.

To summarize, the states have taken varying approaches regarding defining and providing services to gifted children. Each, however, will—or should—have several key components.

- a definition of gifted and talented
- provisions for identification, including nondiscriminatory testing and selection procedures
- procedures for establishing an individualized educational plan (IEP)
- program options, including related services
- procedures for evaluation of programs
- procedures for solving disputes, including mediation and impartial due process
- provisions for awarding diplomas and honors for students finishing high school early
- requirements for school personnel to be considered specialists in gifted education
- financing provisions
- delineation of the responsibilities of local school districts
- transportation provisions

Upon request, state and local agencies should provide all relevant documents that outline the laws, policies, guidelines, rules, and regulations. With or without mandates, influential people—lay and professional alike—are increasingly accepting the idea that gifted children require special educational efforts. There is a growing recognition of the need to identify exceptional children early, and to provide them with opportunities for education of the highest quality all along the way. Those who pursue excellence in education are not likely to settle for less.

References

Educational Amendments of 1974, §404, 20. U.S.C. 1863 (1988).

Jacob K. Javits Gifted and Talented Students Education Act of 1978, §901, 20 U.S.C. 311 (1988).

Karnes, F. A., Stephens, K. R. and Whorton, J. (in press). Certification and specialized competencies for teachers in gifted education programs. *Roeper Review.*

Marland, S.P. (1972). *Education of the gifted and talented (Vol. 1).* Report to the U.S. Congress by the U.S. Commission of Education. Washington, DC: U.S. Government Printing Office.

National Excellence: A Case for Developing America's Talent (1993). Washington, DC: Office of Educational Research and Improvement. U.S. Department of Education. PIP 93-1201.

Renzulli, J.S. (1978). What makes giftedness? Reexamining a definition. *Phi Delta Kappan,* 261.

Stephens, K. R, & Karnes, F. A. (in press). State definitions for the gifted and talented revisited. *Exceptional Children.*

The 1996 State of the States Gifted and Talented Education Report. Council of the State Directors of Programs for the Gifted.

2

The Legal Process and Gifted Education

In our earlier book, *Gifted Children and the Law*, we described in some detail the various components which make up our judicial system. This was not to suggest by any means that all disputes involving gifted children should be taken to court. In fact, we continue to recommend that the formalities of the legal system be avoided if at all possible. Much time, money and emotional grief can be spared if all parties stay clear of lawyers and courts. It continues to be much better for everyone involved to solve disputes through negotiation, mediation, or a due process hearing. Still, as the remaining chapters of this book show, sometimes disputes cannot be resolved without resorting to legal arguments. Therefore, advocates for gifted children need an understanding of legal concepts, court structures and legal terms.

Much of the material discussed in Chapter Two of *Gifted Children and the Law* remains unchanged. America's dual court system consisting of a hierarchical federal and state court structure remains in place, as does the reliance upon state, not federal, law to protect the interests of gifted children. With some notable exceptions, such as cases involving racial discrimination or children who are disabled and gifted, disputes that enter the legal process have remained the province of state judiciaries.

Some parents have attempted to win federal constitutional protection for gifted children under the Fourteenth

Amendment equal protection clause. Such efforts to thus federalize gifted education law, however, continue to be unsuccessful. As noted in Chapter Two of *Gifted Education and The Law*, this approach has been tried without success in the past in *Bennett v. New York (1985)*, and more recently in *Broadley v. Board of Education (1994)*. Judges in both cases refused to grant constitutionally protected status for gifted children.

Federal and state judges (the latter are often required to interpret federal constitutional provisions) instead have seemed content to rely on the three-prong test for Fourteenth Amendment equal protection. This would require gifted proponents to show that they should be protected because there has been (1) a long history of discrimination against that particular class, (2) the attribute involved is easily recognizable, and (3) the possessed characteristic is immutable. While a legal argument can be made for America's long history of cultural ambivalence toward intellectualism, criteria two and three are more problematic. Except when race or gender discrimination is involved, gifted students and their parents so far have lost in the courts when arguing equal protection as a means to obtain access to an appropriate education.

A second type of constitutional challenge has relied upon the words "liberty" and "property" contained in the due process of law clause of the Fourteenth Amendment. This approach has not worked in the courts either. Claims that a student has a liberty right to receive an appropriate education, or that a student has a property interest in receiving gifted education services, have not been persuasive in the courts. Rather, courts have looked to make certain that a student simply had access to an education, and then reasoned it was up to educational administrators how to best serve the needs of the students within a particular district.

In fact, constitutional arguments are so tenuous that it is probably only wise to raise them as supplemental or collateral arguments when there are more specific and substantive claims to assert. One exception to this statement might be with issues regarding the availability of public school gifted services to students who are schooled at home. When home-schooling is undertaken for religious reasons, the First Amendment of the United States Constitution is brought into operation. The religious guarantees of the First Amendment are considered fundamental freedoms in American constitutional law and are given special treatment in the courts.

A problem that continues to perplex persons involved in gifted children disputes is how to secure competent legal counsel. Seldom is there an easy answer. Since most law on gifted children and education is specific to the district and the state, choosing local counsel seems wise. Additionally, selection of an attorney who lives some distance away will add travel and telephone expenses. The following groups might be helpful for those questioning how to proceed:

1. The state gifted association.
2. State, regional, or local bar associations.
3. Gifted education departments located at universities within the state.
4. Law schools within the state.
5. National gifted associations.

Again, we wish to emphasize that settling the dispute at the lowest level is recommended, and if possible, through negotiation or mediation. Proceeding through administrative remedies and keeping disputes out of the formal legal process saves time and money. Additionally, if the dispute ripens to the point that court action is required, courts usually will insist that the parties must make certain that all administrative remedies available through district rules, state administrative rules or statutes, and federal law have been exhausted. For example, the District Court for the Eastern District of New York dismissed a case involving a dyslexic gifted child seeking an appropriate education because the parents failed to exhaust administrative remedies available under the Individuals with Disabilities Education Act (IDEA). The Second Circuit Court of appeals upheld the district court's reasoning for the dismissal of this case *(Hope v. Cortines, 1995)*. No doubt the deficiency in following the IDEA administrative remedies increased costs and delayed any corrective action.

Two new developments, one involving federal government activity and the second involving methodology, require mentioning in this update. The federal Office for Civil Rights (OCR), using civil rights statutes, is actively examining discrimination in the operation of gifted programs. This agency, located in the Department of Education, has become such a major monitor of gifted education that we have added an entire new chapter (Chapter Nine) describing its work. The OCR provides an administrative outlet to settle discrimination claims without going to court and thus provides a valuable resource for parents and school districts to solve problems without, in most cases, resorting to litigation.

The second development concerns the increased capacity to perform electronic research in the law affecting gifted education. As previously noted, gifted education law is primarily state law, with an array of varying agencies being involved in policy and procedures. Thus, attempts to resolve issues means searching administrative rules, statutory law, and often court cases of all 50 states. What used to be a time-consuming task, and one with a great opportunity for error, can now be carried out quickly and with a great deal of precision through computer-assisted legal research (CALR) and the Internet. One caution remains, however. All legal disputes do not become court cases, and all court cases do not result in published opinions. Only when a case reaches a state intermediate Court of Appeals or Supreme court is there the possibility of a published opinion that can be obtained through electronic research. But with new technology, a researcher can be fairly comfortable that he or she has found the latest reported case law relating to gifted youth, the subject matter of the next three chapters.

Court Cases

Bennett v. New Rochelle School District, 497 N.Y.S. 2nd 72 (1985).

Broadley v. Board of Education, 639 A 2nd. 502 (Conn. 1994).

Hope v. Cortines, 69 F. 3d 687 (2nd Cir. 1995).

3

Court Cases and Gifted Students' Educational Opportunities

Although the authors recommend using informal methods such as negotiation, mediation, or administrative hearings to solve disputes, sometimes the only choice for parents is to go to court. This chapter covers court cases that affect the educational experiences of gifted children, updating topics covered in Chapter Three of *Gifted Education and the Law* (Karnes & Marquardt, 1991).

Admission to School

Parents of gifted children seeking early admission to a public school often encounter a statutorily imposed chronological age barrier that prohibits early admission to kindergarten or higher grade. Some state admission statutes do provide some exceptions to a strict age requirement for admission, but most do not, forcing parents who wish their children to have a year of instruction to select a private school.

This problem is a frequent one, although it is a situation that does not produce many reported cases. This lack of case law may be because parents work out an accommodation with the school district, or the case is handled by a court where the decisions are not published in the case reporters, or the child is enrolled in a private setting, or the parents simply wait to start the school experience when the required age is reached. Since school districts are so tightly bound by rather clear statutory language (i.e., the child must be five years old by September 1 to enter kindergarten), the last two reasons probably explain this lack of cases.

A Texas case, *Wright v. Ector County Independent School District* (1993), is a fascinating case in which a mother, Karla Ann Wright, tried to obtain early admission for her son, Brian, into the first grade. Brian had completed kindergarten at an accredited private school, but at age five years and 10 months, was two months shy of being age six on September 1, the age required to attend first grade at a public school in Texas. Ms. Wright presented some excellent arguments, but ran into difficulty because the Ector County Board of Trustees had adopted a blanket policy of no admission to first grade until a child was six years old. Appearances before two meetings of the board did not produce the desired results, and her request for a Texas trial court to issue a *writ of mandamus* (an order to a public official to perform a specific act) directing Brian's admission also was unsuccessful. The trial court also issued a summary judgment in favor of the school district with regard to her claims that she had been deprived of equal protection of the law and due process of law.

Ms. Wright argued six points of error on her appeal to the Texas Court of Appeals, three of which merit discussion. Her first contention was that the Texas statute stating that school boards "may" admit children "either over or under the school age" did not translate into the right to totally exclude children of a certain age. Instead, Ms. Wright contended, the use of the permissive word "may" required the board to hold a factual hearing to determine a child's qualifications for admission. Disagreeing with Ms. Wright's argument, the appellate court stated that in various education statutes the Texas legislature was careful as to how it used this permissive word, and in this case, total exclusion from the first grade of children who had not reached age six was not an abuse of the board's discretion. After all, the court concluded, the board was not banning the children completely from the school system, just from attending the first grade.

The next point Ms. Wright argued is one that arises quite often in admission cases. Texas law, similar to the law in many states, allows a child who has completed kindergarten in another state, but who has not reached age six, to enter the first grade. Ms. Wright contended that this disparity in the admissions procedure was a violation of the equal protection clauses of the Texas and United States Constitutions and thus a violation of 42 U.S. Code §1983. This section of the United States Code allows recovery of damages when a state official acting under state law violates a person's constitutional rights. Ms. Wright contended that the denial of Brian's admission to the first grade, when state law provided for admission of a new state resident less than six-years-old, was discriminatory treatment between two similarly situated individuals. However, she also lost this argument. The appellate court stated that there was nothing in the trial record indicating that the district had ever used this provision of the law, and in addition, the district's blanket prohibition applied to everyone. Furthermore, the court recognized that if Brian was allowed to transfer to the public school and attend first grade at less than age six after completing kindergarten at a private school, he would be given special treatment over the child who attended public school kindergarten and who could not enter public school until age five. There would be no way a public school child could ever enter first grade until age six, which would constitute disparate treatment against public school kindergarten children.

A third argument in this case that influences gifted education law is Ms. Wright's claim that she was denied due process of law under the Texas and United States Constitutions. Although she was allowed to plead her case before the board twice, this type of appearance is much different from an evidentiary hearing where witnesses can speak and the hearing is conducted by an impartial officer. But the appellate court reasoned that there was no need for a formal hearing because of the board's complete ban of admitting to the first grade any child less than six years old. It concluded that a hearing would be a waste of time for both parties.

In the appellate court's opinion that upheld the trial court's refusal to issue the *writ of mandamus* and affirmed the lower court's summary judgment, there was a holding emphasizing how difficult these cases are for parents to win. The appellate court stated that it could not order an issuance of a *writ of mandamus* simply because that portion of the case was moot—Brian was now seven years old. In fact, this may be another reason why so few admissions cases are in the case reports. It takes so long for matters to percolate up through the court system that the child reaches the required chronological age before the matter can be resolved.

Admission to Programs

This section might be more accurately labeled "availability of programs" since it describes the attempts by gifted education supporters not only to garner access to programs, but to get services started so that admission to gifted education would be a possibility. The two cases described in this section are major court holdings in the history of gifted law with, unfortunately for proponents of gifted education, mixed results.

Probably no other case since *Centennial School District v. Commonwealth Board of Education* (1988) has had a greater impact on gifted education law than *Broadley v. Board of Education* (1994). While the case was decided in the Connecticut courts and will have value only as controlling precedent in that state, it illustrates the creative arguments that can be used in court to attempt to win appropriate educational services for the gifted. The case also reinforces the idea that judges, even state supreme court judges, are not going to establish a gifted education program through the interpretation of ambiguous statutes or vague constitutional provisions.

Neil Broadley, a highly gifted student, and his parents sued the Meriden, Connecticut, school district in an attempt to force the district to provide Neil with individualized gifted instruction. Connecticut's gifted education statutes were permissive in nature; that is, school districts had the option of providing gifted education programs, but were not required to offer them. While Neil had received some individualized educational attention, there were no gifted programs in the district.

The Broadleys' major contentions were that the Connecticut constitution and the state's special education statutes created a constitutional right to special education for gifted children. As noted in Chapter Two, these constitutional battles are difficult to win because gifted students have never been designated under the law as a "suspect class," nor has gifted education ever been deemed a "fundamental right." Since the gifted lack these legal protections, a state need not show a compelling interest in treating gifted children differently; instead, to pass a constitutional challenge, a state must only provide evidence that its actions are reasonable. The reasonableness test has a high threshold, and unless the state acts in an arbitrary and capricious manner, the courts will sustain the state's actions.

The Broadleys, however, were able to mount a strong case. As to the relevant statutes, they claimed that the special education statutes classified the gifted as exceptional children, and stated that such children were entitled to individualized instruction because they would be unable to "progress effectively in a regular school program," therefore establishing a statutory right to gifted education. This statutory scheme, combined with Connecticut constitutional language such as "free public elementary and secondary schools," "all men . . . are equal in rights," and, finally, "no person shall be denied the equal protection of the law," constituted a fairly persuasive argument for mandatory gifted instruction. The trial court, however, granted a summary judgment to the school system.

Interestingly, when the Broadleys appealed, the Connecticut Supreme Court transferred the case from the intermediate court of appeals to the high court docket. Evidently, the Supreme Court believed the matter was important and needed resolution by the highest court in the state. Unfortunately for the Broadleys, the court unanimously rejected their arguments, holding that a close reading of the statutes distinguished the state's obligations to the two categories of exceptional children, the disabled and the gifted. For example, statutory language in regard to providing appropriate services to the disabled used the word "shall," while references to furnishing services to the gifted employed the permissive word "may." The mandate to provide services, therefore, applied only to the disabled.

If Connecticut's special education statutory scheme did not support a mandate of services to gifted children, the court concluded that the state's constitution, standing alone, certainly did not do so, either. The equal rights language within the constitution was not controlling, as gifted children did not fall within the suspect class category, thus, making the rational basis test applicable. And, the court held, given the difficulties experienced by many of the disabled, it was reasonable to treat the two groups differently. As to the idea that a fundamental right was at stake, the court decided that education was a fundamental right in Connecticut, but access to gifted education was not. The school door had to be open to Neil Broadley, but he was not entitled to a specific form of instruction.

Although the facts are quite different, *Broadley* bears some legal resemblance to *Bennett v. New Rochelle School District* (1985). In this New York case, discussed in *Gifted Education and the Law* (Karnes & Marquardt, 1991), Richard

Bennett attempted to use the equal protection clauses of the New York and U.S. Constitutions and a general right-to-education clause in the state constitution to win access for Lisa Bennett to a gifted program. The result, however, was much the same as in the Connecticut case. The New York courts were unwilling to provide constitutional protection for a gifted child.

It is clearly very difficult to get a court-ordered remedy for a gifted child unless the district is violating a *specific* statute or administrative rule pertaining to delivery of services to a gifted student. Courts seem unwilling to use vague language in statutes or constitutions to establish gifted education policy.

One of the most fascinating cases in the evolving gifted education law jurisprudence is *Montana Board of Public Education v. Montana Administrative Code Commission* (1992). In this case, it was not a parent suing for the availability of gifted education for children, but an administrative agency suing the state. The results are favorable to the gifted and the opinion is a fine example of judicial craftsmanship.

In 1989, the Montana Board of Public Education adopted the following rule:

> Beginning 7-1-92 the school shall make an identifiable effort to provide educational services to gifted and talented students, which are commensurate with their needs and foster a positive self-image.

The word "shall" in the rule is important because the rule conflicted with a Montana statute, Mont. Code Ann. §20-7-902(1), that stated: "A school district *may* (authors' italics) identify gifted and talented children and devise programs to serve them."

Substantial discussion ensued between the interested parties concerning the conflict between the mandate of the rule and the permissive nature of the statute, including the issuance of an attorney general opinion that the rule was in conflict with the statute and thus invalid. The Administrative Code Committee then requested the legislature to speak directly to the conflict.

The legislature complied, passing House Bill 116 (1991) that included the following provisions:

1. It was the duty of the legislature, not the executive branch, to make the laws.
2. Administrative rules only have the force of law if they are within the powers the legislature has delegated to an agency and the rule does not conflict with a statute.
3. The Board of Public Education mandate rule conflicts with §20-7-902(1), the permissive statute.
4. The legislature affirmed its support of gifted education and encouraged local school districts to initiate identification procedures and implement gifted programs.

Undaunted, the Board went to court, asking for a declaratory judgment that House Bill 116 was invalid as a violation of the separation of powers doctrine. The Board's argument was that the Board of Public Education was given general supervisory powers over the public school system in Art. X §9(3)(a) of the Montana Constitution of 1972. This power was not a power delegated by the legislature to the Board, but instead, a power stemming from the state constitution that could not be changed by mere statute. Therefore, any attempt to change the rule mandating gifted education could not be done by statute but would require a constitutional amendment.

After dealing with some legal technicalities concerning the appropriateness of a summary judgment in this case and the immunity of the Montana Administrative Code Committee (the court found the state to be the actual defendant in the case), the Montana First Judicial District Court agreed with the Board of Public Education that House Bill 116 improperly interfered with the Board's constitutional authority. Pointing out that the

Montana Constitution created three distinct branches of government with designated powers, the court held that the issuance of the rule was well within the Board's constitutional power to exercise general supervision over the public school system. In addition, because the rule emanated from the Board's constitutional power, the Board did not have to follow the requirements of the state's Administrative Procedures Act that established guidelines for adopting agency rules. Interestingly, the court also found unpersuasive a Montana Attorney General's Opinion stating that the Board did not have the power under Mont. Code Ann. 20-1-121 (see content above) to issue the rule. That opinion, the court correctly concluded, focused on statutory law, not the Board's constitutional authority.

There is another aspect of this case of interest to gifted education proponents. As mentioned in Chapter Two, gifted education law is state oriented. Case law is controlling precedent only in the state where the case was decided. However, cases in one states can be argued as a ruling that should be adopted in other states. In the Montana case, the court spent a great deal of time citing the opinion in a West Virginia case, *West Virginia Board of Education v. Hechler* (1988), in which the West Virginia Supreme Court interpreted the power of the state's Board of Education to generally supervise the state's public school system. Under the West Virginia Constitution, the Board of Education had the same constitutional grant of general supervision present in the Montana Constitution. Although the rule contested in the West Virginia case concerned the design and equipment of school buses, the court in *Hechler* concluded that there could be no statutory interference with a rule imposed under the constitutional authority of the West Virginia Board of Education. The situations in the two states were so similar that the Montana court found the West Virginia precedent persuasive.

Two lessons can be learned from the Montana case. One is that even if there are no favorable precedents supporting the gifted in the state, case law in other states that possesses the same factual content and has a favorable outcome might be persuasive to a court. The second is that gifted education proponents may want to look at the structural foundation of their state board of education. The board's rule-making procedure may have a constitutional foundation, and the board might be able to take some important educational steps for the gifted without the possibility of legislative interference.

Admissions and Race

A perennial problem for gifted education programs is to insure that admissions are non-discriminatory as to race, ethnicity, religion, and gender. Of these concerns, the issue of race discrimination appears most often in the case law. In the past, gifted programs came under scrutiny as a segment of a desegregation case against a school district for operating a dual (separation of blacks and whites) school system rather than a unitary one. Many of these desegregation suits are still in the courts and the gifted programs remain under court review.

Two such cases, *Simmons v. Board of Public Education* (1994) and *Keyes v. School District No. 1* (1995), are discussed below. A third case, *Rosenfeld v. Montgomery County Public Schools* (1999), touches upon a topic that may be a common issue as school districts attempt to maintain diversity in their gifted programs—the question of reverse discrimination.

There are, of course, numerous ongoing desegregation cases throughout the country, many of them containing a gifted component. The three cases selected for discussion in this section were chosen because they each have an interesting legal perspective. Since they raise federal law issues, unlike most gifted education cases that are based on state law, they are federal court cases instead of state court cases.

The interesting legal twist in *Simmons* is that the major thrust of the case concerns ability grouping; gifted education, however, also got swept into the legal net. Lou-Ease Simmons, an African-American resident of the Augusta, Arkansas school district, claimed the district discriminated on the basis of race in grouping students by class into low, middle, and high categories, by placing a large percentage of African-American students in special education and Chapter I programs, and by selecting a low percentage of African-American students for the district's gifted and talented program. Her children had participated in special education and Chapter I programs, as all three children required academic assistance. She was not contesting that her children qualified for the gifted and talented program.

The federal district court agreed that the ability grouping was the result of past segregation practices, but did not find that the district currently intentionally discriminated on the basis of race in selecting students for special education classes, Chapter I assistance, or the gifted and talented program. The Judge, Susan Weber Wright, ordered nominal damages to be paid to Lou-Ease Simmons of three dollars (one dollar for each child in the district) and the ending of the ability grouping by class.

Of more interest to gifted education proponents is Judge Wright's review of the alleged discrimination in the gifted and talented program. First, the judge looked at the steady increase in African-American enrollment in the program. Noting that the African-American enrollment had increased from 13% in 1987-88 to 40% in 1992-93 (African-American enrollment in the district was 56%), Judge Wright found that increase to be a substantial expansion of African-American participation in just a few years, though part of this increase resulted from the filing of this lawsuit.

Judge Wright also closely examined how students were selected for the gifted and talented program. Fortunately, for the district, the selection procedures were varied, including referrals by teachers, parents, and the students to a selection committee, and the use of a non-linguistic test, the *Raven Progressive*

Matrices. The district's gifted director also had taken steps to promote the gifted and talented program in the African-American community, and the district had instituted in-service training for teachers to assist in recognizing gifted and talented children. The percentage of African-American students participating, and the extra steps the district had in place to increase African-American participation, allowed Judge Wright to conclude that while in the past the program might have had a segregative effect, at present, the gifted and talented program was not being operated in a discriminatory manner.

Keyes is a very famous case in America's constitutional history. It was in the early rounds of this desegregation suit when the United States Supreme Court held that *de facto* (in fact) segregation, just like *de jure* (by law) segregation, violated the equal protection clause of the Fourteenth Amendment of the United States Constitution. For gifted education proponents, however, the essence of *Keyes* is how the district court in this 1995 round of litigation viewed the racial difference in the district's varied gifted and talented programs.

The court recognized that there were "disturbing" racial/ethnic differences in the district's operation of the gifted and talented, highly gifted, and accelerated course programs. But after making that finding, the court failed to attribute that disturbing difference to racial discrimination occurring 25 years ago. There were, the court concluded, too many societal and socioeconomic factors present to make the causal link to the past racial discrimination. This approach is an interesting legal viewpoint for looking at discrimination in gifted programs.

The court did, however, take a look at many of the same indices of discrimination as Judge Wright examined in *Simmons*. Once again, a quantitative measure was used with the court in finding that African-American and Hispanic participation in the Denver district's gifted and talented program was considerably higher, from a percentage standpoint, than in the African-American and Hispanic participation in gifted programs across the state. The district used a variety of tests, interviews, peer nominations, and monitoring to increase minority participation. Trained gifted teachers were put in elementary schools that had grades three to five, and a Gifted Education Specialist was put in each middle school with one duty being to increase minority participation. As was the case in *Simmons,* procedures were initiated to make minority parents aware of the gifted program and to encourage teachers to recognize gifted minority students. All of these steps, and others, were taken to enhance minority enrollment in all three of the district's gifted programs.

In summary, the court reasoned, the district had shown sensitivity to differences between racial and ethnic groups and had taken steps to equalize participation in gifted programs, but the court realized that some socioeconomic differences between ethnic and racial groups in regard to participation in gifted programs were intractable, and not rooted in the segregation of the past.

Therefore, as long as the district was actively involved in attempts to equalize participation between racial/ethnic groups, the fact that symmetry between such groups had not been obtained did not produce a constitutional violation.

As mentioned above, *Rosenfeld* raises an issue that will likely be a major legal concern in the operation of gifted programs—reverse discrimination. The United States Supreme Court has sent the message through recent case law that any form of minority preferences will be closely scrutinized by the federal courts as a possible violation of equal protection. School districts are often caught in the middle. On the one hand they are pressed to admit minorities to programs to achieve a racial balance, yet on the other hand they face the argument that discrimination against any group, minority or majority, violates equal protection. The Rosenfeld family raised the issue of reverse discrimination within the Montgomery County, Maryland public school system.

At the time the suit was brought, Ethan was a third-grade student who had unsuccessfully applied for admission to the Cold Springs Center for the Highly Gifted. He had good grades and a *Henmon-Nelson Test of Mental Abilities* score that was higher than 12 of the students accepted at Cold Springs. Arielle was a second-grader who had been identified as gifted and planned to apply to Cold Springs.

The Rosenfelds sued the Montgomery County Public Schools, the Montgomery Board of Education, and the school superintendent for injunctive relief and several hundred thousand dollars in damages. Their suit had four counts:

1. Count I sought injunctive relief from all three defendants in their official capacities under the equal protection clause of the 14th amendment.//
2. Count II sought injunctive relief under Title VI of the Civil Rights Act, 42 U.S.C. § 2000 (d).
3. Count III requested $300,000 in damages under the Equal Protection Clause and 42 U.S.C. §1983 from all the defendants in their official capacities.
4. Count IV asked for $300,000 under 42 U.S.C. §1983 from Superintendent Paul Vance in his personal capacity. (This count was not a part of this motion for dismissal).

The defendants filed a motion for dismissal arguing that:

1. Ethan and Arielle did not have standing (a legal term requiring plaintiffs to show they have been injured) to sue as Arielle had not applied to Cold Springs and Ethan, now in the seventh grade, was no longer eligible to attend Cold Springs.

2. The Montgomery County Board of Education was a state entity and protected from suit in the federal courts by the Eleventh Amendment.

The school district lost on the standing argument, with the court pointing out that previous federal court cases had given a broad interpretation to standing when equal protection claims were at issue. In addition, if the district did have a pattern of using lower standards for minority admission to programs, as the Rosenfelds alleged, that policy would affect the children's future opportunities within the system as they would not be on equal footing with all others in the application process.

The immunity issue revolved around whether the Montgomery County Board of Education, when acting in its official capacity, was a state entity protected from suit in a federal court by the Eleventh Amendment, or whether it was a local agency not shielded from suit. Basing its decision on past Maryland case law, the court held the Board was a state agency and thus immune from federal suit for money damages. Count III, therefore, was dismissed in its entirety.

Citing a famous United States Supreme Court precedent, *Ex Parte Young* (1908), the court found, however, that members of the board acting in their official category were subject to prospective relief through the issuance of an injunction and refused to dismiss that portion of the case. The requests contained in Count I for injunctive relief against the Montgomery County Public Schools and the Board of Education were dismissed, but the board members acting in their official capacity were subject to an injunction. The Court also refused to dismiss Count II, citing a history of cases where the Eleventh Amendment was inapplicable to requests for injunctions in federal courts under the Civil Rights Act, 42 U.S.C. §2000(d).

At the time of this writing, *Rosenfeld* is in its preliminary phase. Even at this incipient stage, however, the Rosenfeld claims send a message to persons involved with gifted education programs. If there is differential treatment based on racial considerations, the school district must be ready when faced with statutory and constitutional challenges to validate its selection process. For example, taking as a fact the Rosenfeld claim that Ethan's academic record and test score exceeded that of 12 persons admitted to the gifted program, how would the Montgomery district justify Rosenfeld's rejection? Establishing in writing sound selection procedures (perhaps reviewed and approved by a credible agency outside the school district), following those procedures, and keeping detailed records, will be essential to withstanding a legal challenge. Given the political and philosophical debates over whether affirmative action has a role in today's society, there will certainly be future court challenges to race-based admissions procedures.

Curriculum Modification

Suits involving curriculum modification are the most common type of gifted education dispute. Parents believe their children are not receiving appropriate instruction and school districts are not being responsive to their concerns. Therefore, parents, acting in behalf of their children, take their dispute through the administrative channels and finally reach the courts. Usually, this process takes several months, if not years, and a considerable amount of time and money.

Huldah A. v. Easton Area School District (1992) is a typical modification case. It arose in Pennsylvania, a state that mandates gifted education and statutorily defines both gifted and disabled children as people in need of special education. By placing gifted children in the special education category, Pennsylvania provides them many, but not all, of the state and federal substantive and procedural protections that safeguard the disabled. Given this legal framework, a large number of gifted education cases reach the Pennsylvania courts.

The Easton Area School District had two programs in place to assist intellectually gifted students. In the early grades, gifted students participated in a pull-out program where they left the regular classroom to attend a class session composed entirely of gifted students. When gifted students reached the eighth grade, they, along with other qualified but not necessarily gifted pupils, were placed in specific courses that made up the district's enrichment program. Huldah's father, Drew Anderson, objected to the enrichment program approach, requesting that she be kept in a pull-out program. Unsuccessful in negotiating a solution with the district, he began seeking administrative relief.

After a due process hearing, the hearing officer ordered the district Multidisciplinary Team to write a report for the Individual Education Program Team to assist in determining Huldah's educational requirements. The hearing officer refused the father's request for the district to pay for an independent evaluation of Huldah and did not address the request for attorney's fees.

Drew Anderson then appealed to the Special Education Appeals Panel, a state entity established to hear appeals from hearing officer decisions. The panel agreed with the hearing officer that the district did not have to pay the expense for an independent evaluation and that Huldah should be kept in the pull-out arrangement until completion of the assessment of her educational needs. This group did address the Anderson petition for attorney's fees, ruling that the panel did not have jurisdiction to order their recovery.

An appeal to the Pennsylvania Commonwealth Court did not provide the family much relief. The court upheld the Special Education Appeals Panel conclusions that the Andersons could not recover attorney's fees or the expenses they had incurred in supplementing Huldah's education during these proceedings. There is language in the court's opinion, however, particularly

Judge Byer's concurring opinion (an opinion that agrees with the outcome of the case but for different reasons than those expressed in the majority opinion), that takes the district to task for not being more responsive to the Andersons' procedural requests. Particularly on point was Judge Byer's insightful comment:

> *It truly is unfortunate when the proper education of a gifted child must be determined through an adversarial litigation process. A court is not the best forum for deciding such issues. Instead, for the education system and the administrative review process to function properly, there must be more cooperation by school districts in addressing the legitimate concerns of parents of gifted children than occurred at least initially in this case.*

The next two cases are also from Pennsylvania and deal with an issue not addressed in the authors' previous writings—compensatory education for gifted students. One case, *Punxsutawney Area School District v. Dean* (1995), upheld an award of compensatory education, while in *Brownsville Area School District v. Student X* (1999), such a remedy was denied.

Melissa Dean, a seventh-grade gifted student in the Punxsutawney system, complained that attending school at the Jefferson Building was causing her to suffer respiratory problems and other illnesses. Her parents asked that she be transferred to another building, but the district refused to make the change. Instead, the district placed Melissa in homebound instruction where she remained for 30 days.

Upon her return to school at the Jefferson Building, Melissa's illnesses continued and she obtained a pediatrician's opinion that she should be either transferred to another location or assigned to homebound schooling. Despite the physician's recommendation, the district refused the transfer and Melissa remained out of school for two months, receiving no instruction. At the end of this period, the district issued a Notice of Recommended Assignment (NORA), again placing Melissa in homebound instruction, but the notice was backdated 30 days. The parents refused to sign the NORA and requested a due process hearing.

Astonishingly, the hearing was extremely protracted. The hearings were held over six sessions in a three-month period. It was not until seven months after the hearing was requested that the hearing officer rendered a decision that contained the conclusion that there was no link between Melissa's physical symptoms and the Jefferson Building. There was no specific evidence, the hearing officer concluded, that her education environment had a "substantial impact" on her educational experience. Interestingly, the school district had received a similar complaint from the parents of a disabled child who charged that their child also physically suffered from attending classes in the Jefferson Building. The district dismissed that complaint, which then matured in the court suit, *Kanouff v. Punxsutawney Area School District* (1995).

An appeal by the Deans to the Special Education Appeals Panel brought a reversal of the hearing officer's decision on procedural grounds. The panel found that the district, contrary to the Individuals with Disabilities Education Act and Pennsylvania state law, erred 1) by failing to give the Deans notice and information concerning the district's actions and 2) by the district's failing to evaluate Melissa to determine what steps needed to be taken to provide her with an appropriate education. As a remedy, the panel ordered the district to evaluate Melissa, provide notice to the Deans as to what actions were being taken, and finally, provide compensatory education of four days a week from February to the end of the school year. This compensatory education could be completed by taking summer courses or some other enrichment schooling.

The district appealed to the Pennsylvania Commonwealth Court on two grounds, one being that since the hearing officer had found that Melissa had no physical or mental disability, and the appeals panel did not overrule this finding, the district did not have to abide by the legally required notice and information procedures. Second, the district claimed that it had complied with the federal and state law notice and evaluation requirements.

Neither of the district's arguments was persuasive to the court, which found that the district had not provided a rationale to the Deans for its action in ignoring Melissa's request for a change in buildings, nor had the district provided any data to show that homebound placement was the least restrictive environment for Melissa. Both failures violated state and federal law. In addition, the court found that compensatory education was the appropriate remedy for such violations and the fact that the district provided a due process hearing for Melissa did not satisfy the district's procedural and substantive obligations to Melissa. There was, the court pointed out, no quarrel with the manner in which the due process hearing was conducted; instead, it was the lack of accommodation to Melissa's educational and physical needs prior to the hearing that violated her right to an appropriate education.

The case involving Student X illustrates how important legal precedent is in gifted education litigation. Student X was highly gifted, ranking in the top 5% of all kindergarten students in the nation in math, reading, and language. Yet, despite parental inquiries to the district as to the availability of accelerated and enrichment programs for their child, he received no specialized instruction until the fifth grade. When Student X reached the fifth grade, the district did establish an Individualized Education Plan (IEP) for a gifted program, but had no individualized plan for specific students. Five years later, the parents again became concerned as to their child's curriculum and requested an IEP for Student X, but refused to sign the plan submitted by the district. Instead, they requested a due process hearing.

The hearing officer found that the district was not providing a free and appropriate education for Student X and ordered the district to provide the child with an individualized education plan and 1,954 hours of compensatory education which could be completed up to six years after completion of high school and could include college-level work. When the district appealed, Pennsylvania's Special Education Appeals Panel upheld the hearing officer's decision.

The district's appeal to the Commonwealth Court was more successful. Using the language of *Centennial,* the court held that the Special Education Appeals Panel had exceeded its authority by stating that the compensatory education could include work at a college or university. While the court referred to the *Punxsutawney* case that declared compensatory education a proper remedy when a district failed to provide an appropriate curriculum for a gifted child, it used the *Centennial* precedent to find that the remedy proposed for Student X could not go outside the available curriculum within the school district. Therefore, post-secondary school remedies, private tutors, and any remedy outside the district's present curricular offerings could not be part of the compensatory education package. Once again, a court used the negative language of the *Centennial* opinion to limit a gifted education opportunity for a student.

Gifted Children with Disabilities

A new type of conflict has appeared on the legal landscape the past few years—cases where a child is both gifted and disabled. Because the protections for the disabled under the federal Individuals with Disabilities Education Act (20 U.S.C. §1410) are more inclusive than state laws protecting the gifted, these cases usually cite violations of the federal act and are filed in federal courts. But the gifted issues in these cases often significantly affect outcomes as shown in *Conrad Weiser Area*

School District v. Department of Education (1992) and *Fowler v. Unified School District No. 259* (1995).

May a child who meets the requirements to be designated as gifted also be in need of special education services? Yes, said a Pennsylvania court, because the child may need help in reaching the student's intellectual abilities. The parents of Samuel L. requested that the Conrad Weiser School District provide special education for their child who had difficulty completing written work. The district thought that Samuel could be accommodated in the regular classroom, and both parties agreed to submit the dispute to a hearing officer who concluded that the child did not have a learning disability requiring special education.

When Samuel's parents appealed to the Special Education Appeals Panel, that body concluded that Samuel did have a learning disability and did need special education services. The district then took the case to the Pennsylvania Commonwealth Court, which ruled in favor of the parents' request. How and why they did so could have a notable impact in the development of gifted education law.

One of the school district's arguments was that Samuel was so successful in the regular classroom that his achievements precluded his receiving special education. But the court focused on a section of Pennsylvania law (22 Pa.Code §342.1 (ii)) that said a person is in need of special education if there is a "condition that manifests itself as a severe discrepancy between achievement and intellectual ability in one or more of the following areas: . . . (C) written expression." This section of the code was a key factor because the appeals panel had found that Samuel had a learning disability in written expression. This finding, combined with the district's stated recognition of his intellectual ability and high I.Q., suggested a discrepancy deserving of special education services. The court rejected the district's argument that under Pennsylvania law only those children who deviated from the average in mental characteristics should receive special education services. Instead, the court held that the panel recognized that for Samuel to succeed in the regular classroom, despite his high intellectual ability, he was going to have to have special instruction in writing.

The Fowler case involved Michael, a profoundly deaf ten-year-old child whom the district determined had "superior intellectual capacity." Unfortunately, the district, although having designated Michael as gifted, provided no gifted education services for him. Therefore, his parents enrolled him in Wichita Collegiate, a private school, and asked that the district provide interpretive services for Michael. The district refused, stating that its policy was to cluster hearing impaired children at Caldwell School so deaf special education services could be provided in an efficient and practical manner. The district also asserted that its policy was to provide interpretive services all day for deaf children in the district and this would not be economically feasible for one child at a private school. The district did provide a gifted education consultant who met once a month with Michael's teacher at Wichita Collegiate.

In 1995, a new individualized education plan (IEP) was created for Michael which, among other things, recommended that he have 180 minutes per day in a gifted resource room. The district said it would create this resource room at Caldwell. However, since Michael would be the only one to use it and would not have the advantage of interacting with other gifted students, his parents requested a due process hearing.

Basing his decision on federal and Kansas law, the hearing officer concluded that the district must provide interpretive services for Michael at Wichita Collegiate. In Kansas, hearing officer decisions are reviewed by a district review officer who, in this case, reversed the hearing officer's decision. The applicable law, the review officer reasoned, required that services be provided equally to special education services, and since children in the public schools did not receive interpretive services on a one-to-one basis, Michael should not have such access either. A federal court, however, viewed the applicable law differently.

Cost and practicality arguments, the court determined, were superseded by the needs of the student. The school district would not have to pay Michael's tuition to the private school, but it did have to provide special education and related services. Federal law required such services to both public and private school students and Michael, despite the district's concern for administrative practicality, was entitled to receive interpretative services. Other hearing impaired students attending other schools within the district had received individual interpreters and Michael, although attending a private school, by law must receive the same special education services. The fact that the district had provided individual interpreters to children in the public schools revealed that it was not an administrative or economic impossibility to provide such assistance.

The above cases are representative samples of the curriculum modification cases that have reached the courts in the past decade. There is no doubt such cases will continue as the courts attempt to weigh the needs of a gifted child with the economic resources of the district. Several of the above cases reflect that balancing. For example, Student X may receive compensatory education as a court-imposed remedy, but the compensatory instruction can be confined to the district's curricular offerings, saving the district untold expenses for tutors and college tuition. On the other hand, economic concerns of the district did not, in the Kansas court's view, supersede the student's needs in *Fowler.* No doubt such legal and economic balancing will continue to occur in the courts as we enter the first decade of the new millennium.

References

Bennett v. New Rochelle School District, 497 N.Y.S. 2d 72 (1985).

Broadley v. Board of Education, 39 A. 2d 502 (Conn. 1994).

Brownsville Area School District v. Student X, 729 A. 2d 198 (Pa. Commw. Ct. 1999).

Centennial School District v. Commonwealth Board of Education 539 A. 2d 785 (Pa. 1988).

Conrad Weiser Area School District v. Department of Education, 603 A. 2d 701 (1992).

Ex Parte Young, 209 U.S. 123 (1908).

Fowler v. Unified School District No. 259, 900 F. Supp. 1540 (D. Kan. 1995).

Huldah A. v. Easton Area School District, 601 A. 2d 860 (Pa. Commw. Ct. 1992).

Keyes v. School District No. 1, 902 F. Supp. 1274 (D. Colo. 1995).

Montana Board of Public Education v. Montana Administrative Code Commission, Cause No. BDV-91-1072 (Unreported case, 1992).

Rosenfeld v. Montgomery County Public Schools, 41 F. Supp. 2d 581 (D. Md. 1999).

Simmons v. Board of Public Education, 843 F. Supp. 1296 (E.D. Ark. 1994).

Punxsutawney Area School District v. Dean, 663 A. 2d. 831 (Pa. Commw. Ct. 1995) (The *Punxsutawney Area School District v. Karouff* case is a companion case with *Dean* and can also be located at this citation).

West Virginia Board of Education V. Hechler, 376 S.E. 2d 839 (W. Va. 1988).

Wright v. Ector County Independent School District 867 S.W. 2d 863 (Tex. App. Ct. 1993).

4

A Case-By-Case Look at School Policies

Affecting Gifted Education

This chapter discusses new cases concerning school policies and laws affecting students and teachers. The format parallels that in Chapter Four of *Gifted Children and the Law*, though new cases have not emerged in every section covered in the previous work. In some areas, however, there have been several extremely significant cases, particularly those dealing with busing, tuition, and teacher certification.

School Policies and Students

Two Pennsylvania cases, *Ellis v. Chester-Upland School District* (1994) and *New Brighton Area School District v. Matthew Z.* (1997), upheld school district decisions not to provide busing to gifted students who were asking for transportation to gifted programs offered outside the school system. The cases also involved tuition and attorney's fees.

Monique Ellis, a first grader at Holy Ghost Catholic School, was identified as a gifted student and her mother, Maxine Brown, requested that the Chester-Upland School District pay a portion of Monique's tuition and all of her transportation costs to Tower Hill, a private school in Delaware. The school district performed a multidisciplinary evaluation and concurred that Monique was a gifted student.

The district then convened Ms. Brown, her attorney, the principal of Holy Ghost, and the district's school psychologist to develop an individualized education plan (IEP) for Monique at a public elementary school. The plan included placing Monique in an itinerant support gifted program, one where the teacher of gifted children travels from school to school within the district. It was recognized that the IEP committee had no member who was qualified to draft an IEP for a gifted student, and so Ms. Brown rejected the plan. The district then requested that Ms. Brown prepare an IEP to accompany the district's "part time itinerant/support" plan. Ms. Brown prepared her plan based upon the curriculum of Tower Hill and requested a tuition amount of $695.00 (Monique had a scholarship from Tower Hill covering 91 percent of her tuition) and transportation costs.

A hearing officer sided with Chester-Upland, stating that the district had provided an appropriate plan for Monique, that the district's gifted education teacher could implement the IEP, and that there was no right to tuition and transportation costs. In Pennsylvania, a hearing officer's finding is appealable to a Special Education Due Process Appeals Review Panel, and Ms. Brown took advantage of her right to challenge the hearing officer's decision. The panel upheld the hearing officer's finding, and Ms. Brown, having exhausted her administrative remedies, sued the district in Commonwealth Court.

In court, Ms. Brown lost her battle on two fronts. First, the court concluded that there was no evidence presented at the due process hearing that Monique required a full-time gifted program, nor was there evidence presented that the district did not have the resources to provide her with appropriate instruction. Second, even if the program provided by Chester-Upland was not appropriate, Pennsylvania law does not provide for tuition payment for gifted students to attend private schools or for out-of-state placement. There were opportunities for Pennsylvania public school children to be placed in private schools or out-of-state institutions, but these circumstances were specifically outlined by statute, primarily covering students with severe disabilities. The court, therefore, upheld the panel's decision denying tuition, transportation expenses, and Ms. Brown's request for attorney's fees.

The *New Brighton* case expanded the opinions found in the *Ellis* case. In the case of *New Brighton Area School District v. Z.*, the mother of Matthew Z., an eleventh grade gifted student, wrote an IEP that included science and computer courses at a nearby college. The IEP was constructed at a meeting that included the school's guidance counselor and several others. There was no mention by any of the parties as to who would pay the tuition and travel costs to attend Geneva College. When the mother sought reimbursement for the costs, the district refused to pay. A hearing officer upheld the district's denial of payment and concluded that a new IEP for Matthew should be developed. Acting upon the mother's appeal, the Special Education Appeals Review Panel reversed the hearing officer and ordered the district to reimburse the mother for the courses. New Brighton then took the matter to court.

The Pennsylvania Commonwealth Court reversed the Special Panel, saying that a public school district has no legal obligation to reimburse a parent for college expenses. Instead, citing the seminal case in gifted education, *Centennial School District v. Department of Education* (1988), the court concluded that a school district needs only to provide an appropriate education for a student within that district's curriculum. School districts should not be forced to pay for tutors or individual programs outside the district's offerings, the court stated. Such a compulsion, the court determined, would "constitute more than a free appropriate public education."

Both cases are setbacks for gifted education advocates. While both cases cited *Centennial*, the court in *New Brighton* seemed ready to stretch the language of *Centennial* and be the least supportive of gifted education. The two major findings of the Pennsylvania Supreme Court in *Centennial* were that pull-out programs were not always sufficient to meet the needs of an individual student, but that a school district did not have to become a Harvard or a Princeton to maximize a student's abilities. Shortly after the *Centennial* decision, Marquardt and Karnes (1989) surmised that the decision was a two-edged sword for gifted education supporters—helpful in its emphasis on the IEP and individualized instruction, but dangerous in its language that limited the definition of what was an appropriate education for a child in all circumstances to resources present in the school district's curriculum and instructional staff.

School Policies and Teachers

Several cases in this chapter illustrate problems gifted education teachers encounter working in the profession. They are typical problems involving accidents (accidents involving students in gifted programs are discussed in Chapter Eight), transfer of duties, seniority, and certification. They are included here not only for their description of the substantive law problem involved, but also for their insight into the operation of the legal system. In one case involving age discrimination, legal procedure trumps the substantive right claimed, supporting the contention of the authors that litigation is a precarious process and should be avoided if possible.

Gifted Teachers and Scope of Employment Claims

Is a teacher traveling to and from a gifted conference in a private automobile acting under the scope of her employment and thus covered by workers' compensation? It depends on the facts, states the Nebraska Supreme Court in *Reynolds v. School District of Omaha* (1990). Tragically, the facts and Nebraska law did not support the case of Karen Reynolds, a gifted facilitator in the Omaha schools.

Mrs. Reynolds traveled from Omaha to Lincoln to attend a two-day gifted education conference. On the last day of the conference, she drove from her Omaha home to the conference site. On her way back, she passed the exit to her home, picked up her sister, and drove to her school, where she copied articles from the conference, fed her gerbils, and watered plants. She then drove her sister back to her workplace and started home. On the way home, she was involved in a car wreck that left her disabled.

A three-judge workers' compensation commission denied her compensation, finding that the accident did not occur within the scope of her employment. The Nebraska Supreme Court agreed, stating that the case fell under the "going and coming rule," that is, employees traveling to and from work are not acting within the scope of their employment. In this case, the Court refused to apply the "special errand" theory that Mrs. Reynolds was traveling under an order from her employer at the time of the accident, or to utilize the traveling salesman approach that covers employees as long as they are away from home and acting in a business capacity. Interestingly, a dissenting judge believed that Mrs. Reynolds should be covered until she returned home from her business trip.

This decision did not mean that Mrs. Reynolds could not pursue a remedy, if possible, from an insurance carrier or a negligent driver. It simply meant that she would not have access to the financial strength of a workers' compensation award. However, the case is one that gifted teachers who regularly attend professional conferences using private transportation might wish to keep in mind and take steps to make certain they are financially protected.

Another case involving a gifted teacher's occupational injury had a different outcome in *Lorentzen v. Industrial Commission of Arizona* (1990). Upon her employment as a teacher of the gifted in the district's high, middle and primary schools, Ms. Lorentzen told school district officials that she was highly allergic to pesticides and could not accept the employment unless she was promised she would not be exposed to chemicals that caused her to have a reaction. Notice to administrators was particularly important since her duties not only required her to visit several school buildings, but the district also furnished an apartment for her. Shortly after her employment, the teacher began suffering blurred vision and other allergy symptoms that became progressively worse to the point where she could not talk. At the recommendation of her immunologist, she resigned her position.

An administrative law judge employed by the Arizona Industrial Commission found that Ms. Lorentzen's illness, although suffered through the course of her employment and while living in the apartment, was not compensable because she could have suffered the affliction if she not been employed by the school district. According to the administrative law judge, her disease was not peculiar to her specific duties as a gifted education teacher and was an ordinary disease common to the general public.

Ms. Lorentzen's appeal to the Arizona Court of Appeals was more successful. That court accepted her argument that her illness was the result of an accidental exposure to pesticides suffered under the course of her employment. Such accidents arising during the course of employment were compensable under

Arizona Workers Compensation Law. The requirement for Ms. Lorentzen in future legal actions, the court stated, would be to show that she was injured by an accidental exposure to pesticides.

The significance of this case is that teachers should warn employers of special health situations and that school districts must live up to agreed-upon accommodation policies. Where there is sufficient evidence to show that the employer did not abide by a promise tendered, the district could be held liable.

Transfer

Transfer of teachers from gifted education to the regular classroom often, but not always, causes hard feelings due to a variety of reasons. Perhaps a teacher's love of working with the gifted student, a teacher's perceived loss of status, or applicable language within an employee's contract, would make such transfers legally difficult. The case, *Zotos v. Lindbergh School District* (1990), depicts a situation where a transfer was contested and a teacher's attempt to remedy the situation became lost in an arcane legal maze.

Katherine Zotos began teaching in the Lindbergh schools in 1965. In 1985, she began teaching in the district's gifted and talented program and continued until March 27, 1990, when she was notified that she would be transferred to a regular third grade class. Expecting that she was being discriminated against because of her age (53), Ms. Zotos filed an age discrimination complaint on July 19, 1990 with the Equal Employment Opportunity Commission (EEOC). On November 14, 1990, the EEOC issued a right to sue letter stating that she had two years to file an age discrimination suit or three years to file if the employer had acted with willful discrimination.

In March 1991, Ms. Zotos was transferred back to the gifted education program but two weeks later was reassigned to the third grade classroom. On June 21, 1991, she notified the district that she would take early retirement. She then filed a second complaint with the EEOC arguing that she had suffered a "constructive discharge," a legal claim that one has been forced out of a position. Again, the EEOC issued a right to sue letter (dated January 23, 1992) and informed Ms. Zotos that the rules had changed regarding the law for filing a lawsuit. The new rules required a lawsuit 60 days after the charge had been filed with the EEOC, or 90 days after the receipt of the EEOC's action.

Ms. Zotos filed suit against the school district in federal district court on June 26, 1992. The school district's answer to the suit contained the affirmative defense that Ms. Zotos' case was barred by the statute of limitations, although the district did not specify whether it was relying on the 90 days or two-year limitation. The federal district court accepted the general language of the school district's pleading and dismissed the case. Ms. Zotos appealed to the Eighth Circuit Court of Appeals, arguing that the lack of specificity in the statute of limitations defense did not justify the district court's summary judgment against her. She also on appeal raised the claim that her treatment was willful discrimination and the three-year statute of limitations applicable in willful discrimination cases should apply. The court of appeals did not agree with either argument. That court ruled that the standard language in the district's answer constituted a sufficient affirmative defense, and, citing precedent, that her treatment did not fall under the legal definition of willful discrimination. The court of appeals upheld the district court's assessment of approximately $5,000 in legal costs awarded to the school district.

Since this case was decided by a summary judgment on procedural grounds, it does not provide a great deal of insight into the legal aspects of transferring teachers out of gifted programs. The case does provide guidance as to the need for pursuing appropriate administrative remedies, when applicable, as Ms. Zotos did by registering a complaint with the EEOC and obtaining the right to sue letters. It also illustrates the need to make certain that all legal remedies are timely pursued, or the substance of the case may be thwarted by procedural rules.

Seniority

The question of seniority often arises in gifted education, particularly in states that do not require certification or specialized training for gifted education teachers (Karnes and Marquardt, 1994). Unless state regulations govern who may be in the gifted education classroom, should a history teacher with greater seniority replace a teacher who is conducting a successful gifted education program? Two Pennsylvania cases illustrate the problems that may occur.

In *Dallap v. Sharon City School District* (1990), a gifted education coordinator was retained while teachers who had more seniority were caught in a staff reduction and dismissed. The gifted coordinator possessed an English certificate, but she did not have, nor did the job require, certification in gifted education. The teachers who lost their positions argued that all the teachers had the same level of certification and thus the reduction should be based on seniority. The district's superintendent stated that it would be "educationally unsound" to replace the gifted education coordinator who evidently was doing an excellent job. The school board and two Pennsylvania lower courts upheld the retention decision, but the Pennsylvania Supreme Court, despite acknowledging that the trial record indicated that the gifted coordinator was extremely qualified, held that the district had to adhere strictly to the state seniority statute. The court did not accept the premise that since the position did not require certification, the district had discretion in filling the post. Instead, the court concluded that the lack of any specialized certification or job qualifications made the seniority test the principal factor.

A second Pennsylvania seniority case, *Dilley v. Slippery Rock Area School District* (1993), had a different outcome. Although the facts were similar to *Dallap* (i.e., the school district was experiencing a declining enrollment and teachers on the staff had greater seniority than the retained gifted education faculty member), there was in *Dilley* a major intervening factor. Kathleen Nachtman, the gifted education teacher, possessed a program specialist certificate from the state's Department of Education. This certificate was a credential requested by the school district for a gifted education teacher working in a school system. The gifted education position also called for expertise in computers, a skill possessed by Ms. Nachtman. Dilley, an industrial art teacher who had more seniority but no program specialist certificate or computer training, sued the district claiming that he should be placed in the gifted education slot. Certainly, based on the three-year-old *Dallap* precedent, he appeared to have a strong case. The Pennsylvania Commonwealth Court, however, distinguished *Dilley* from the holding in the *Dallap* case by stating that in *Dallap,* all the teachers had the same level of certification. Because Nachtman possessed the program specialist certificate and computer training, the court concluded that a strict application of the seniority rule was inappropriate.

The lesson of these two cases seems to be that even when there is no gifted certification requirement in the state, gifted education teachers should seek specialized training. The training should be of such a nature that a third party would recognize it as providing a particular competency in gifted education. This will allow courts to cite this training so that they may deviate from a strict seniority rule.

Certification

Twenty-eight states require specialized courses for certification in gifted education. (Karnes, Stephens, Whorton, in press). *Gifted Education and the Law* (Karnes & Marquardt, 1991) discussed *Johnson v. Cassel,* a 1989 West Virginia case in which that state's court of appeals ordered a school district to replace an uncertified hire for a gifted program with a person possessing gifted education certification.

Since the reporting of that case, a second West Virginia certification case, *Egan v. Board of Education* (1991), has been litigated and reinforced the *Johnson* decision. In *Egan,* the Taylor County School District had an opening for a person to teach gifted education for grades five through eight. The person selected had a bachelor's degree, experience teaching the gifted and disabled, experience in substituting in the district, and certification to teach grades one through six, but held no certification in gifted education. Sarah Egan, who was not selected for the position, had 14 years of teaching experience, a Master's degree, certification in grades kindergarten through eight, and was in the process of obtaining gifted education certification. When Egan sued the district, the trial court concluded that there were sufficient strengths in the educational background of the hire to prevent setting aside the selection as an abuse of the school board's discretion.

For several reasons, the West Virginia Court of Appeals disagreed with the trial court. The appellate court found that Ms. Egan had greater qualifications plus work toward gifted education certification. In fact, by the time the case reached the appellate court, she had received her gifted education certificate, a point the court noted in its opinion. The court's opinion was a strong one, not only ordering that Ms. Egan be hired, but also awarding her back pay and other work-related benefits, the costs of bringing the action, and reasonable attorney's fees.

Summary

Several conclusions can be reached from the cases in this chapter. Most importantly, as illustrated in *Ellis,* it is essential that the law on the subject be thoroughly researched before pursuing litigation. For example, if state law does not allow payment for gifted students to attend private schools or tuition to out-of-state schools, it is unlikely an appellate judge will alter the statutory policy. Most judges are prone to leave financing issues to the legislature and not amend education policy. Likewise, judges are not likely to ignore an applicable statute of limitations. It is a major sin to allow a procedural law to prohibit a substantive issue from being litigated. Admittedly, the question of which statute of limitations would apply in *Zotos* was somewhat confusing, but litigants need to make certain that deadlines are met.

In some cases, such as the *Reynolds* case, the law may be less clear, leaving room for judicial interpretation. Litigation, therefore, is necessary to flesh out what legal theory the judges will apply. Unfortunately for Karen Reynolds, the court selected a theory unfavorable to her position. If the stakes are large enough, however, it is worth the legal cost to test the waters, a strategy employed in several cases in Chapter Eight.

References

Karens, F.A. & Marquardt, R.G. (1991). *Gifted education and the law: Mediation, due process and court cases.* Scottsdale, AZ: Gifted Psychology Press (formerly Ohio Psychology Press).

Karnes, F.A. & Marquardt, R.G. (1994). Gifted education and the courts: Teacher certification and employment decisions. *Roeper Review,* 229-231.

Karnes, F.A., Stephens, K.R. & Whorton, J.E. (in press). Certification and specialized competencies for teachers in gifted education programs. *Roeper Review.*

Marquardt, R.G. & Karnes, F.A. (1989). The courts and gifted education. *West's Education Law Reporter, 50,* 9-14.

Court Cases

Centennial School District V. Commonwealth Department Education, 539 A. 2d 785 (Pa.1988).

Dallap v. Sharon City School District, 571 A. 2d 368 (Pa.1990).

Dilley v. Slippery Rock Area School District 625 A.2d 153 (Pa. Commw.1993).

Egan v. Board of Education, 406 S.E. 2d 733 (W. Va. 1991).

Ellis v. Chester-Upland School District, 651 A. 2d 616 (Pa. Commw. 1994).

Johnson v. Cassel, 387 S.E. 2d 553 (W. Va. 1989).

Lorentzen v. Industrial Commission of Arizona, 790 P.2d 765 (Ariz. Ct. App. 1990).

New Brighton Area School District v Matthew Z., 697 A.2d 1056 (Pa.. Commw. 1997).

Reynolds v. School District Of Omaha, 461 N.W. 2d 758 (Neb. 1990).

Zotos v. Lindbergh School District, 121 F. 3d 356 (8th Cir.1997).

5

Negotiation in Gifted Education

As parents and others are confronted with disputes regarding gifted children and their education, a beginning step in the process of resolving an issue is negotiation (Karnes, Marquardt, and Troxclair, 1997). This informal procedure begins at the heart of the conflict and proceeds along administrative channels. Screening and identification issues usually begin with the coordinator of gifted programs, the school assessment team or school psychologist. Placement situations will sometimes start with those people who have specific administrative responsibilities. Instructional inequities usually initially rest with the teacher.

To be prepared for negotiation, one must first have the total picture on what is permissible for the gifted student. Copies of the state laws related to gifted education, the state board policies and those at the local, county, or parish level will provide valuable information about permissible alternatives. It is imperative to have these in writing and not to have the information based on hearsay and misinformation. If there have been related court cases or due process hearings, these should be reviewed, if they are not privileged information.

Usually a letter or phone call to the local board of education office and the state department of education will prompt quick dissemination of printed information. The state association for the gifted is another source of reliable printed information. The process used within a specific district may be disseminated through a parent handbook published by that district.

In the negotiation process, establish a paper trail in the form of a letter at the very outset, indicating the reasons for coming together and the time and place of the meeting. After the meeting, another letter should be sent requesting verification of the outcome of the meeting and stating a reasonable amount of time (usually five working days) for a response regarding results or the next steps to be taken. If the meeting's outcome is favorable, written documentation will help insure that the discussion results in appropriate action being taken. However, if the outcome is not positive, the letter will be a useful record and the basis of taking the issue to the next level of resolution. Also, keep written records, including summaries, of telephone calls. Meticulous record keeping may be cumbersome, but it is necessary (Karnes, Troxclair, and Marquardt, 1997).

Be sure to have a clear picture of the chain of command within the school district. In seeking resolution of an issue, you may need to continue upward from the teacher to the principal, assistant superintendent, superintendent, and then the school board. These steps may change somewhat depending on the conflict and the size of the school district. Be sure to formally schedule appointments and follow each meeting with a letter summarizing the key points discussed and outcome(s) of each individual meeting. Depending on the issues, legal counsel may be desirable, but usually is not necessary at this level.

In order to speak at a school board meeting, the official request to be on the agenda usually must be made in writing several days prior to the specific date. As throughout the negotiation steps, be sure to present facts, not opinions, in a non-emotional manner—thoroughly and with courtesy. Whatever decision the board makes, request that it be stated in writing in a timely manner. In some cases, a written request may have to be made for written confirmation of a decision, whether positive or negative.

Being informed through printed copies of laws, rules and regulations, and policies will assist in the negotiation process. Staying positive and pleasant helps establish an atmosphere of collaboration. Always create a paper trail and follow the educational chain of command. These are the key ingredients to positive negotiations.

We understand, however, that not every issue will be resolved at this initial stage simply through negotiation. The more formal processes of mediation and due process may be necessary. Thus, it is wise to have information pertaining to these, in case the dispute is not resolved through negotiation.

References

Karnes, F.A., Marquardt, R.G., & Troxclair, D.A. (1997). The evolving legal framework in gifted education. *Understanding Our Gifted,* (9), 2, 3-5.

Karnes, F.A., Troxclair, D.A., & Marquardt, R.G. (1997). Parents and the legal rights of gifted children. *Parenting for High Potential,* March, 20-22.

# Gifted Education and Mediation

In 1993, Karnes and Marquardt reported that approximately ten states offered formal mediation as a source of solving disputes in gifted education. By 1997, the number increased to twenty-one (Karnes, Troxclair, & Marquardt, 1998).

Mediation in other areas of education has been mandated and generally implemented, and the concept of formal mediation is widely known. Under the provisions of the federal law, Individuals with Disabilities Education Act of 1997, all disabled students in the United States have the right to mediation. For the parents and teachers of the gifted who have exhausted the negotiation process from the point of the dispute going along administrative lines through the superintendent and on to the local school board level, mediation is a viable vehicle for finding a resolution in the most friendly, amiable manner. In the states where a recognized mediation process is available, the procedures are relatively easy to follow.

The Mediation Process

The first step is to contact the appropriate agency, usually the department of education, at the state level. Although procedures vary somewhat across the twenty-one states, mediators are usually appointed from the state level and, after a formal request has been received, will contact the party of need to determine the appropriate time and place for the mediation meeting.

The characteristics and knowledge of the mediators are very important to the success of the process. They must be excellent communicators in the written, speaking and listening processes. Positive interpersonal skills are necessary to facilitate a productive and pleasant meeting environment. Mediators should have formal training in the process of mediation and should be knowledgeable regarding all laws, rules and regulations in the area being mediated—in this case, gifted education and related areas.

The person representing the school district at a mediation hearing must have the authority to make commitments to all agreed solutions. Both parties must bring suggestions for the best resolution of the issue(s), and both should have positive attitudes. Although attorneys may be present for each party, their presence is not necessary in most situations. On occasion, the gifted student may be present.

The process begins with the mediator asking each party to present its side and perceptions of the dispute, along with any documentation. Then the mediator meets individually with each party and asks questions which should be helpful in resolving the problem. When each believes a solution is forthcoming, a mediation agreement is written to be signed by each party. The agreement should be very specific in terms of what must be accomplished, who is responsible for each step, and the time line involved. In *Gifted Children and the Law*, Karnes and Marquardt (1991a) have offered specific examples of well written and poorly constructed mediation agreements. If the mediation process does not result in agreement, and does not produce a signed agreement, the parties may then proceed to a due process hearing, if available for the gifted, or whatever other options are attainable within the state.

Current Status of Mediation in Gifted Education Across States

Karnes, Troxclair, and Marquardt (1998) reported that mediation for gifted students is available in twenty-one states, either at the state level or through local options. Mediation is an option through legislative action or statutes and regulations in six states (Alaska, California, Kansas, New Mexico, Pennsylvania, and South Dakota). Six states (Alabama, Connecticut, Louisiana, Nevada, Oregon, and Tennessee) provide mediation at the state level for students under special education and include the gifted. In Connecticut, however, mediation is only available in regard to the identification of these students. Nine states (Arkansas, Hawaii, North Dakota, Michigan, Utah, Virginia, Washington, West Virginia) and the District of Columbia have mediation as a local option for gifted children and youth.

Mediation Resources

Karnes, Troxclair, and Marquardt (1998) have also identified several resources which could be assets in implementing mediation. The Departments of Education in several states have published materials describing the mediation process. Written mediation guidelines that describe the process, the roles of both parties, and the procedures for scheduling a meeting are described in printed materials available from Connecticut. A brochure and a question and answer packet are provided by the Oregon Department of Education. Guyer (1995), Hicks (1995), and Kay (1995) also have described how mediation has positive results in resolving disputes, the merits of the mediation process, and how to avoid due process.

Alaska has a written law incorporating mediation, Sec. 14.30.193, School District Hearings Subsection (c). Written guidelines concerning mediation within Alabama are available in Supp. No. 93-3. Tennessee likewise has written procedures and other helpful handouts regarding participants, roles, checklists and forms to use in the mediation process. All of these can be obtained by writing the respective state departments of education. Specific information concerning the process of mediation can be found in *Gifted Children and the Law* (1991a) where Karnes and Marquardt have offered detailed descriptions of all of the steps of the mediation process including a model agreement.

Recommendations

Despite its increased use, mediation is still not sufficiently available in many parts of the country. State and local associations for the gifted and talented, state and local bar associations, state departments of education, faculty of colleges and universities, and other advocates need to be proactive in espousing the positive aspects of mediation (Karnes, Troxclair, & Marquardt, 1998). Mediation can be a particularly helpful tool in avoiding costly and time-consuming litigation, and needs to be used more widely regarding education provisions for gifted children.

Even in those states that recognize mediation, it tends to be underutilized. Newsletters, letters to the editors, brochures, videotapes, e-mail chains, and other print and non-print public relations tools should be employed to inform parents and all schools of the availability of the process. State departments of education should conduct quality training, not only for potential mediators but also staff development for parents of the gifted and school officials. These training sessions could be conducted in conjunction with local and state bar associations. Similarly, state associations for the gifted can continue to update their members with keynote and concurrent sessions on the topic through conferences and workshops.

For those states or localities that do not have mediation available, a study of the laws and rules and regulations of other states will reveal the best components to incorporate in a state. A special committee could undertake not only the analysis of the gathered information, but also the best procedures for the establishment of mediation at the state level. Questions to consider may be:

- Is there a state law that could be amended to include mediation?
- Should a separate bill be written and what legislative support would be necessary for the introduction, debate, and passage of this bill?
- What are the opportunities to have mediation approved by the state board of education without the passage of a statute?
- Are there provisions by which the mediation process may be adapted by local education boards without a state law or rules and regulations of the state board of education?

Mediation is a viable, informal mechanism for solving disputes. However, less than half of the states have the procedure in place for gifted children and youth. With proper advocacy and a plan of action, perhaps the remaining states will be able to facilitate this positive, informal procedure for solving disputes in the near future.

References

Guyer, R. (1995). Mediation works. *Sail, 10,* 14.

Hicks, G. M. (1995). Procedure matters: Avoiding due process hearing. *Sail, 10,* 1, 5-6.

Kay, K. (1995). Mediation: A positive step in conflict resolution. *Sail, 10,* 1, 3.

Karnes, F. A., & Marquardt, R. G. (1991a). *Gifted children and the law: Mediation, due process, and court cases.* Scottsdale, AZ: Gifted Psychology Press.

Karnes, F. A., & Marquardt, R. G. (1991b). *Gifted children and legal issues in education: Parents' stories of hope.* Scottsdale, AZ: Gifted Psychology Press (Formerly Ohio Psychology Press).

Karnes, F. A., & Marquardt, R. G. (1993). Pathways to solutions: Using conflict resolution in matters of gifted and talented. *Gifted Child Today,* 38-41.

Karnes, F. A., & Troxclair, D., & Marquardt, R. G. (1998). A survey of mediation opportunities in gifted education. *Gifted Child Today,* 46-48.

7
Gifted Education and Due Process

Due process is a procedure in which an aggrieved party has the right to present facts that will be heard by an impartial hearing officer (Karnes, Troxclair, & Marquardt, 1998). When a dispute cannot be settled at the school district, the local board of education level, or through mediation (both previously described), due process proceedings are a logical next step. Almost half of the states have a provision for procedural due process regarding gifted education.

During the due process procedure, both parties may or may not want to be represented by legal counsel. The parents have the right to choose whether or not to have the child present, and they may say whether the hearing should be open or closed to others. Each party has the right to have the proceedings recorded and to receive a copy of the report written by the hearing officer within forty-five days after the meeting.

There are several different provisions among the states which have due process for gifted children. Alabama, Alaska, Florida, Kansas, Louisiana, New Mexico, North Carolina, Pennsylvania, Tennessee and West Virginia have the same provisions for the gifted as those set forth regarding disabled children. Connecticut provides due process only as applied to the identification of the gifted. South Dakota has a due process provision specifically focused on gifted children. A general due process procedure, but one that is applicable to gifted children, is available in the District of Columbia, Montana, and Texas.

Not surprisingly, the various states have significant differences as to the initial hearing level, jurisdiction, the selection and training of the hearing officers, and the appeals routes (Karnes & Marquardt, 1991a). However, there are several common elements in due process across states. They all provide that a written notice must be given to the participants saying that a hearing has been scheduled, and this notice must state the time and place as well as the name of the hearing officer. Another commonality is the opportunity to present evidence, witnesses, and oral arguments, along with the option of having legal counsel. Additionally, all due process hearings must be recorded either orally or in written form. Also, the hearing officer must forward in a timely manner a written decision based on the arguments and evidence presented at the hearing.

Karnes, Troxclair, and Marquardt (1998) reported that within and across states, there is a wide variance as to the format, detail, structure, and writing style represented. The procedural due process reports regarding gifted children were first analyzed by Karnes and Marquardt in *Gifted Children and the Law* (1991) where 70 hearings were reported. The specific issues were varied, involving screening and identification, appropriate placement, school district transfers, etc. An additional study on due process by Karnes, Troxclair, and Marquardt (1998) revealed twenty-six hearings in seven states during the time span of 1992-1995. The primary issues were: appropriate placement and/or programming, program eligibility and/or identification, compensation, and a few categorized as miscellaneous. Pennsylvania had the highest number of due process hearings (13), followed by Tennessee (8). Indiana, Louisiana, New Hampshire, North Carolina, and West Virginia each reported one.

Appropriate Placement and Programming

Appropriate educational placement and provision of programs for gifted students comprised a large percentage of due process cases. In Pennsylvania, a state that recognizes the need for individualized educational programming (IEP) for gifted children, the hearing officer decisions in eleven of the thirteen cases focused on appropriate placement and programming. Three of these hearings were very similar in nature and all involved services to the gifted being provided by the school librarians. Two hearings focused on the appropriateness of programming and special education procedures for two ten-year-old girls. The hearing officer concluded that the Individualized Educational Programs (IEP) for these two girls had to be modified to include instruction in art therapy. The hearing officer also stated that interruptions needed to be eliminated in the library by having someone to take over the general duties of the librarian who needed to devote full attention to the gifted students. Further, the officer ruled that all IEP conferences would need to have a Local Education Agency person present when discussing and writing the plans.

An eleven-year-old gifted male was also being provided services by the librarian. The results were similar with the hearing officer requiring the addition of mathematics and science programming. The elimination of interruption during the gifted education time frame in the library was also stated in this IEP.

Sometimes the hearing officer simply ruled that an educational placement was not appropriate, but left it to the school personnel to devise more appropriate placement and/or programs. The parents of a gifted girl, age eleven, were concerned regarding the appropriateness of the IEP and the hearing office stated that a new one had to be written.

Another due process hearing had a different outcome. After reviewing their fifteen year old daughter's gifted program and being dissatisfied, her parents requested that she be placed in another district. The hearing officer determined that the current school district was capable of writing and implementing an appropriate IEP, and that in-service training be given to the regular classroom teachers responsible for implementing it.

In a more complicated case, the parents of a gifted student with an attention deficit disorder and learning disabilities alleged that the district had violated procedural processes, and they contested the implementation of the program that was being provided by the district for their child. They requested psychotherapy, compensatory education, and reimbursement for the costs of previous testing and for a drama class attended by their child. The hearing officer denied all parent requests. This ruling was upheld by the appeals panel when the parents filed for exemptions. The parents were, however, granted psychological testing and a new IEP for their child.

In another due process hearing, the parents questioned a second administration of an intelligence test, the grade placement of their child, and appropriateness of the IEP. The hearing officer ruled that fifth grade was an appropriate level for the child, but that upon mastery of the appropriate material, the student would be accelerated to the next level. The current IEP was ruled appropriate to meet the instructional needs of the child.

One hearing involved parents who maintained that the public school's current programming was inappropriate, that the appropriate placement would be in a private school, and that the public school had failed to adhere to procedural safeguards for the education of the child. They requested reimbursement for tuition and transportation expenses to that private school. Tuition reimbursement for private schooling was denied, as was transportation. The public school programming was deemed to be appropriate, and the hearing officer concluded that no procedural safeguards had been violated.

However, the IEP had to be rewritten to clarify the meaning of enrichment and acceleration.

In another situation, the hearing officer determined that a course in desk top publishing and one in computer graphics, both requested by the parents, as well as an honors English course, would be appropriate educational experiences for that gifted child. Transportation for those classes should be provided as well, the hearing officer concluded.

Mathematics was the subject of two additional hearings. One involved an eight-year-old. The hearing officer ruled that the needs of the student could be met through homogeneous grouping within the regular classroom. However, the district was cited for two procedural errors in sending a notice of assignments to the parents before the IEP meeting, and the hearing officer concluded that proper representation from the district was not at the IEP meeting.

The other due process hearing involved an eighteen-year-old gifted student whose IEP was challenged. The parents had requested reimbursement for college tuition, transportation and textbooks. The decision stated that the parents could pay for the above mentioned items or that the student could complete the necessary course in his high school.

Tennessee, like Pennsylvania, provides for gifted children under the same provisions as they do for disabled and has had two hearings pertinent to appropriate placement and programming. One situation ended with the decision to record a grade obtained in a college course by a junior high student on the high school transcript of the boy. In another decision, the hearing officer determined that a student with above average ability and achievement could be placed in the gifted class only if the scores met the proper criteria. The issues of appropriate placement and programming in gifted education appear to be ongoing with increases in the number of hearings.

Program Eligibility and Identification

Karnes and Marquardt (1991) pinpointed identification and program eligibility as being particularly serious areas of concern. The following were reported by Karnes, Troxclair, and Marquardt (1998) and include several hearings from 1992-1995.

In Louisiana, a non-qualified young child had been denied admission to a program for the gifted, and the hearing officer upheld the decision of the district. In North Carolina a decision in favor of the district ruled that the student was properly identified, that an appropriate IEP had been written, and that the school had not denied free and appropriate public education. The parents were denied reimbursement for private school placement.

In a West Virginia hearing, a gifted child had been identified as gifted in one state, but was denied admission when moved to another state. The parents brought to the hearing the issues of adequacy and appropriateness of the evaluation instruments, their rights to an independent evaluation, the validity of certain intelligence tests, and claimed discrimination in the use of instruments other than the WISC-R (*Wechsler Intelligence Scale for Children-Revised*). The hearing officer ruled the evaluation was appropriate and that eligibility requirements were not met. The officer further stated that the parents could have private testing at their own expense, and that those results would have to be considered by the eligibility committee. The hearing officer also stated that it was not within his/her scope to regulate which test must be used for eligibility and identification.

In Pennsylvania, the hearing officer upheld the decision of the IEP team to deny eligibility of a second grade male student for the gifted program. Although the child's test scores were sufficient to qualify as a gifted student, it was determined that the regular classroom teacher could provide enrichment activities and classes in his areas of strengths.

Although these various due process rulings are not ones that will necessarily please parents, it is still important that they know what the current rulings tend to be. Certainly, identification is a fundamental issue. If a child is not correctly identified as having special educational needs, then a school may not know what programs are needed to meet those needs.

Compensation

The question of compensation occurs occasionally in court. In one Tennessee case, the issue was reimbursement for a psychological examination, and for free and appropriate public education. The hearing officer stated that the school system must have their Multidisciplinary Team reevaluate the child through the school psychologist and, based on those findings, appropriate action must be taken.

Reimbursement for the costs of private schooling and for identification of a twelve-year-old as seriously emotionally disturbed were issues in another hearing in Tennessee. The hearing officer's finding was that the child should be moved from a public school to a private day treatment facility/school for the 1992-93 school year with the current IEP to be implemented in that placement, and with the school system paying all expenses. For the 1993-94 school year, the child would be moved to a different public school from the one previously attended, and there would be a change in classroom grouping and a new IEP. A settlement for compensation for tuition and mileage was established.

Miscellaneous

Several issues do not fall within the above categories but deserve some attention. In a Pennsylvania decision, the hearing officer determined that the standard mastery level for admission into a gifted program in a particular school was at the 92nd percentile for elementary students in that school. This level differs from those apparently used most often throughout the country—the 95th through the 97th percentile—and represents a determination of eligibility based heavily, if not exclusively, on percentile scores.

In Tennessee, one hearing involved many issues. The parents claimed that their child's student rights had been violated due to the assessment team's noncompliance with previous agreements. There were questions concerning whether the assessment conducted prior to determining eligibility was comprehensive and valid, and whether the psychologist performed them in a professional and ethical manner. Additional issues focused on questions of observational data, an integrated written assessment report, composition of the evaluation team, and whether required assessment data were provided. The hearing officer ruled that a team knowledgeable about the need for a reevaluation would meet within fourteen days. The ruling required that the team must include a reevaluation of vocational assessment, and, if gifted services were warranted, the issue of transportation must be determined.

In another Tennessee hearing, the issue involved a school's ruling that because a student had not participated in the marching band, the student was not "in good standing" and thus could not participate in All State Band activities. The parents' wishes for the student to participate prevailed. The band director was instructed to certify to the appropriate organization, the Middle Tennessee School Band and Orchestra Association, that the student was in good standing and should be allowed to audition for the Mid-State Honors Band.

The parents had also claimed that the school district had failed in several ways to provide related services at the home school, had not provided for the student's right to privacy, and had failed to provide to them written notification of any modification in the child's program. They had also claimed unethical conduct on the part of a school counselor. The officer dismissed these charges, ruling that they did not have a factual basis for having any kind of relief under state special education law.

New Hampshire and Indiana each had one hearing. The New Hampshire situation involved the home-schooling of a gifted student after the school refused to change the classroom placement because the parents had not followed the proper procedures for doing so. Despite the many demands by the parents for such things as a computer, piano lessons, textbooks for home-schooling, and an exception to take the GED early, the hearing officer ruled in favor of the district and denied all the parental requests. In Indiana, the parents wanted a substitution of previous test scores for current test scores in determining the placement in a biology class of a learning disabled student with above average ability and achievement. The decision of the officer stated that the student could be placed in the class only if the current scores met the criteria.

The issues of appropriate placement and programming in gifted education appear to be ongoing, and the number of hearings is increasing. We anticipate that this trend will continue as parents become more knowledgeable regarding their rights.

Summary

We would like to once again point out that when issues cannot be resolved through other procedures like negotiations or mediation, due process, if available, provides a viable and usually preferable alternative to going to court. It is not as expensive, nor as protracted over time. Due process hearings usually take place within a forty-five day time line and do not include the interruptions experienced in court cases such as discovery, completing interrogations, filing motions, and scheduling the judge and the court room, to name a few extenders of time (Karnes, Troxclair, & Marquardt, 1998). The emotional dynamics are usually less. The cost in terms of money with attorney's fees, court costs, and the possible loss of wages due to being in court do not come into play. In addition, the formal rules of evidence do not apply in a due process hearing, although either party may have an attorney present.

As we noted previously, not every state allows formal due process to be used in situations involving gifted children. In those states without the benefit of due process for the gifted, every effort should be undertaken to have it in place. State association and other groups may wish to seek an amendment of a state law, the state rules and regulations, or policies and procedures. The state board of education may wish to establish a policy, or the local, county, or parish board may agree to accept the concept. Ideally, the state law(s) pertaining to the gifted should provide for due process.

A model for the development and implementation of guidelines for due process is contained in *Gifted Children and the Law* (Karnes & Marquardt, 1991). This model includes recommendations for statewide staff development for teachers, administrators and other school personnel, parents and concerned citizens. In addition, the model urges the establishment of a statewide record system for the purpose of analyzing issues for possible changes and corrections in law and/or regulations and policies.

At the risk of being overly repetitive, we must again state that due process provides a less complicated and adversarial method for resolving issues pertaining to the gifted than going to court. States with due process may wish to review their standards and those without it may want to strive for it.

References

Karnes, F.A. and Marquardt, R.G. (1991). *Gifted children and the law: Mediation due process, and court cases.* Scottsdale, AZ: Gifted Psychology Press (formerly Ohio Psychology Press).

Karnes, F.A., Troxclair, D., and Marquardt, R.G. (1998). Due process in gifted education. *Roeper Review, 20* (4), 297-301.

8

Other Legal Issues Related to Gifted Youth

Gifted children are often placed in situations where they find themselves in harm's way. They attend residential and day programs, participate in field trips, and travel to off-campus instruction. Unfortunately, as discussed in Chapter Five in *Gifted Education and the Law*, deaths and serious injuries have occurred to some students attending gifted programs. This chapter discusses three accident cases not included in the authors' earlier research.

These cases reinforce the maxim that persons who offer gifted programs must take steps to minimize risks. For the safety of the children, the success of the program, and the staff's own financial well-being, a great deal of preventive work needs to be undertaken to avoid injuries. Several ideas for the preclusion of injuries are discussed at the end of this section.

A child's giftedness is also an issue in domestic relations matters. If a child support agreement directs the father to pay for a college education, should that education be at a state university, or a prestigious and private one? Should child support payments be increased by a court because a child is identified as gifted and wishes to attend an expensive school that has an extensive gifted curriculum? Should educational opportunities for gifted children in the geographic area where each parent resides be a factor in child custody decisions? These kinds of family law issues, and other similar questions, appear amazingly often in the court reports. So frequently do they occur that only a sample can be discussed here.

Accident Cases

Perhaps no better case illustrates a school district's failure to foresee a potential injury than *O'Campo v. The School Board of Dade County* (1991). School authorities told eleven-year-old Angelina O'Campo to be at Coral Way Elementary School at 6:55 a.m. in order to be picked up and transported to South Miami Elementary School to attend a special arts program for gifted children. School authorities did not take into account that Coral Way was not open at that early hour and there was no staff present to supervise her. One morning, while waiting for her transportation to the gifted program, she was attacked and raped.

In responding to her suit against the school district for recovery of damages for physical, mental, and emotional injury, the school board contended that they had no duty to protect Angelina from criminal acts by third parties. The district also argued that they had no prior notice that such violent acts might occur, as there had been no similar incidents at Coral Way. Despite the O'Campos' contention that the district had a duty of care to Angelina by instructing her to be at the school, the circuit court judge granted the school district's motion for a summary judgment.

Not surprisingly, the Florida Court of Appeals reversed the trial judge and remanded the case to the trial court. The appellate court stated that the school district had a general duty of care to a child when the district was entrusted with the care of a child. In this case, such a duty of care and supervision was created when the school authorities told Angelina to be at the school at 6:55 a.m. The appeals court concluded that whether this created duty had been breached was a question for jury determination and so the case was returned to the trial court.

The accidental explosion in a chemistry laboratory at Ben W. Murch School in the District of Columbia was briefly discussed in Chapter Five in *Gifted Children and the Law* (Karnes & Marquardt, 1991). Reference was made in that chapter to Stewart Ugelow's account of the pain and suffering he experienced as a result of that explosion as published in Jill Krementz's work, *How It Feels to Fight for Your Life* (1989). A second case stemming from that accident is now in the case reports, *District of Columbia v. Howell* (1992). The case should be required reading for anyone involved with a gifted program.

Like Stewart, Dedrick Howell was attending the Murch Summer Discovery Program and was seriously injured in the accident, suffering burns on his hands, arms, face, and chest. When the explosion occurred, the eight-and nine-year-old children were making sparklers as a "hands on" experiment under the direction of a chemistry teacher. Dedrick had to undergo several surgeries, rehabilitation therapy, and psychotherapy, as well as future medical treatments.

Dedrick and his parents sued the District of Columbia and The American University (the director of the program and the chemistry teacher were both Ph.D. candidates at American, and the chemicals came from American) in the Superior Court of the District of Columbia, winning a ten million dollar judgment. The jury awarded Dedrick eight million dollars for pain and suffering and two million dollars to the Howells, one million for loss of parent-child consortium (right to share normal activities with child), and one million for future medical expenses.

The jury found the defendants liable under several legal theories: 1) the Murch principal had failed to exercise ordinary care for the children in the summer program; 2) the director of the program, who was acting as an agent for the District, failed to exercise ordinary care for the safety of the children; 3) the chemistry teacher's negligence, although he was acting as an independent contractor, was attributable to the District; 4) both the director of the program and the chemistry teacher violated District of Columbia regulations against manufacturing fireworks; and 5) the District's permitting the presence and use of dangerous chemicals failed to maintain the school grounds in a safe manner. The District of Columbia and American University were held to be jointly and severally liable.

American University settled with Dedrick and his parents, but the District of Columbia appealed the trial court's judgment to the District of Columbia Court of Appeals. At the appellate level, the District was successful in overturning the two million dollar award to the Howells. Evidently the loss of parent-child consortium was not recognized as a legal basis for recovery in the jurisdiction and the appellate court found there had not been sufficient evidence present as to the specificity of future medical costs. Dedrick's eight million dollar judgment, however, was upheld.

The review court pointed out that the trial court could have found the District liable on any of the five theories mentioned above. The appellate court focused on the number three, the chemistry teacher acting as an independent contractor employed by the district. Normally, employers are not liable for the negligence of an independent contractor, but District of Columbia law included a provision making employers liable when the contractor is employed to do work involving a special danger to others.

The appellate court concluded that there was sufficient evidence that the facts in this case fit the special danger exception. The children were quite young, they were asked to wear goggles during the experiment, and most important, the chemicals involved included potassium perchlorate, a highly unstable chemical that is used to make rocket fuel. Because of its volatility, potassium perchlorate is not used in the manufacture of commercial sparklers. It was an easy call for the court, in this case, to hold the District vicariously liable for the actions of the chemistry teacher. Since liability under this special danger exception to the no-liability-of-independent contractors doctrine was so clear-cut, the appellate court did not consider the other four theories of recovery.

Of interest to directors, staff, parents, and students involved in gifted programs is the tangled web of legal relationships in this case. First of all, the program was held in an elementary school belonging to the District. The principal of Murch school received approval from an assistant superintendent to offer the program, and the principal had selected the director. The director hired the staff, including the chemistry teacher, although the principal interviewed all members of the staff and had veto power over the selection of teachers for the summer program. All in all, there seemed to be sufficient connection between the District and those people operating the program to establish the District's liability. If the appellate court had not used the employer-independent contractor approach to decide liability, these relationships would have been extremely important, as the District would be the only one of the parties capable of paying such a large judgment.

A second interesting legal aspect of the case was that during the initial trial, the District sued as third-party defendants (a procedure that allows all issues involved in a case to be decided at one trial) the director, the chemistry teacher, and a staff person who were all assisting in the experiment. The chemistry teacher was declared bankrupt and dismissed as a party, the staff member was found not negligent, but the director had a judgment entered against him for contribution to the District's financial liability.

A third case, *Moore v. Tucson Electric Power Co.* (1988), is interesting in that an Arizona appeals court, affirming a trial court decision denying damages, cited a child's intellectual ability as a reason for denying his recovery for injuries. Michael Moore, acting as guardian for 14-year-old Brooke Burwell, brought an action against Tucson Electric Power Company. Brooke had climbed a pole, watched a sunset, and then attempted to traverse the power lines to an adjacent pole. When he touched uncovered metal wires, he was knocked unconscious and fell to the ground. In a previous climb of the utility's poles, he had walked on bare metal wires and not been shocked.

Moore's claim was that the location of the power poles and uncovered metal wires in an alley where children played created an "attractive nuisance." Attractive nuisance is a tort law doctrine recognized in many states that allows property owners to be liable for negligence if there is a condition on their property that causes physical harm to children. The power company countered that the doctrine should not apply because Brooke fit the trespasser definition under Arizona law which meant they had no tort liability.

One of the aspects of the Arizona attractive nuisance doctrine was that an owner could be liable if the children, because of their age and experience, did not recognize the condition or realize the risk imposed by the dangerous condition. For two reasons, the appeals court held that the attractive nuisance doctrine did not apply in this case. The court's first rationale was that a power pole is not easily climbed and it takes a considerable amount of effort to reach the top of the pole. Most children would not be casually attracted to the top of a power pole.

The second reason was more applicable to the developing law relating to gifted children. The court noted that Brooke, who attended a high school for intellectually gifted students, was of superior intelligence and that he excelled in mathematics and science. Therefore, given his experience and knowledge, he should know the dangers of touching uncovered wires on power poles and the attractive nuisance doctrine should not apply. Instead, the court treated Brooke as a trespasser and the appellate court affirmed the decision of the lower court that the utility company was not liable for his injuries.

All three of the accident cases above contribute to the developing body of law relating to gifted children. Each case sends several legal messages to people working with gifted children.

For example, *O'Campo* illustrates that people operating gifted programs have a clear standard of care to those people under their supervision, even if the duty is created in a minimal fashion. Issuance of a mere directive was sufficient to trigger a legal standard of care.

O'Campo also illustrates the duty of those involved in gifted programs to foresee dangerous conditions. Placing a child on a school ground without supervision at 6:55 a.m. created a foreseeable risk to the child. It is the moral and legal obligation of persons in charge of children to identify potential injuries to a child, regardless of the source of the danger, and take steps to alleviate those risks.

Howell presents several warnings to parents and program directors. It is important to know the substance of the curriculum of a program. Was it appropriate for eight- and nine-year-old children to make sparklers? The principal of Murch, for example, testified that she had never seen children of such a tender age wearing goggles when performing an experiment. The added negligence of the use of a highly dangerous chemical turned this section of the curriculum into a physical and mental tragedy for the children, and an eight million dollar financial disaster for the school district.

The *Howell* case also depicts the financial plight program employees may suffer if they commit negligence or some other legal violation. There is a tendency for injured parties to sue all individuals who are potentially liable and let the courts weed out the people who can provide a viable defense. Even if a staff member is not found liable, providing the cost of a defense can be financially devastating. It is essential that people not only protect children from injuries, but also take steps to prevent themselves from financial ruin.

Both Dedrick Howell and Brooke Burwell (the pole climber) encountered an idea often held by adults, and one that is frequently injurious to gifted children—that intellectually talented children should be treated as adults. People often fail to realize that while children may be able to perform sophisticated computer applications or complete problems in advanced calculus, they possess many of the normal physical, mental, and emotional characteristics of their chronological age. The thought of eight- and nine-year-old children mixing chemicals using a mortar and pestle to make an incendiary device seems inappropriate, but, perhaps it would not be for high school children. For an adult to use supporting wires to climb a power pole, touch bare lines, and then claim utility liability for injuries would be ridiculous. For an intellectually curious 14-year-old to do so might not be such a legal stretch. Gifted children are smart, but in legal matters, they are children, not adults.

Domestic Relations Cases and the Gifted

As noted above, it is surprising how often the intellectual and artistic talents of a child become a significant issue in a domestic relations case, particularly in child support and child custody cases. While in most of these cases, a judge considers several factors in making a decision "in the best interest of the child," the cases below describe instances where the fact that the child was gifted played a contributing role in the outcome.

Child Support

Requests for extraordinary child support for the gifted child typically fall into three categories. Quite common is a request to provide for a child's special needs, such as music lessons, travel abroad, field trips, or tutors. A second group of cases involves switching the gifted student from a public to a private school, and a third issue relates to the funding of a gifted child's college education. Examples of all three case categories are discussed below.

Special Needs

To obtain some consistency in child support awards within a state, all states have legislatively or judicially mandated guidelines for awarding child support. Ann Umstot persuaded a Tennessee trial court to deviate from the state's child support guidelines and award her an extra $1,000 payment in order to send her daughter to Europe. *Umstot v. Umstot* (1997) was a distinct victory for gifted children because the Tennessee Court of Appeals, in upholding the lower court's award, gave permission for trial judges to adjust the guidelines upwards for private school tuition. A second major ruling was that the appellate court stated that the choice to send a child to a private school was the prerogative of the custodial parent. In many support cases, private school enrollment for a gifted child is often a contentious issue between the custodial parent, who is often in a position to see the need for such education, and the noncustodial parent designated to pay child support, who, in many cases, is focused on monetary concerns.

A North Dakota court in the case of *Addy v. Addy* (1990) also agreed with the plea of the custodial parent that the intellectual abilities of her children warranted an increase in child support. Patricia Addy argued that she experienced increased educational costs because her son was intellectually gifted and her daughter was a talented musician. These facts, along with other claims, helped her convince a trial judge and the North Dakota Supreme Court that increasing intellectual promise shown by her children constituted a material change in circumstances in raising the children to warrant an increase from $250 per child to $600 per child per month.

The Tennessee appeals court found no abuse of discretion by the trial court in increasing the child support payment, *Scott v. Scott,* (1988*).* Lack of money kept Kelly Scott from participating in a gifted program, belonging to a book club, performing in a talent show, and taking part in gymnastics and dance activities. Her mother used these arguments and others to win an increase in child support from $250 per month to $100 per week.

Private Schools

In *Gifted Children and the Law,* the authors discussed an Alabama case, *Howard v. Howard* (1974), where a mother was able to win an increase in child support based on the intellectual promise of her children. Key to that outcome was an admission by the father during the proceedings that private schooling was "probably a good idea."

Just the obverse stance was taken by a New Jersey father in the 1994 case, *Hoefers v. Jones.* William Jones argued that his First Amendment and New Jersey religious freedoms were violated if he was ordered to continue to pay tuition for his two children at a private Christian school. Under the terms of the divorce settlement, William had agreed to pay $500 per week child support and the 1991-92 private school tuition for his children to attend King's Christian School.

Janet Hoefers had residential custody of the children, but the parents had joint legal custody. Under the terms of the divorce agreement, both parents were to be involved in the major health, education, and general welfare decisions of the children, B.J. and W.J. As to the tuition payments subsequent to the 1991-92 school year, the divorce agreement set out conditions for future tuition payments. Seemingly, all these conditions were met by Janet, who sent grade cards and school work to William, offered to meet with him on a monthly basis to discuss the children's schooling, and, in a timely fashion, sent William the tuition coupon payment books. Despite these efforts, William contested paying the tuition for the 1992-93 and 1993-94 school years and the upcoming 1994-95 term.

William, an agnostic, claimed that his paying tuition to King's Christian School constituted an involuntary support for religion. Furthermore, William correctly contended that the divorce settlement contained language requiring both parents to agree before he was obligated to make tuition payments to a private school. Consequently, he ordered his attorney to notify Janet that he would not pay the 1992-93 tuition.

The Superior Court of New Jersey handled the constitutional issues easily, citing a long line of cases where the best interest of the child doctrine trumped a constitutional claim. The payments were not supporting religion, the court concluded, but were contributing to the educational well-being of his two children, who were "thriving educationally." New Jersey law required that, as a parent, he provide schooling opportunities for his children, and the private school tuition was the means used to accomplish this responsibility.

William's contention that the contract language of the settlement required mutual agreement for the tuition payments following the 1991-92 school year was a more difficult hurdle for the court. It leaped this hurdle by stating that when joint legal custody was in effect, it was the duty of the parties to communicate regularly concerning major decisions affecting the children. William had unilaterally ceased communication with Janet and the children and thus was prohibited by the "unclean hands" equity doctrine (a principle that a person seeking relief in a court must be free of any wrongdoing) from using the court to end his liability for the past tuition payments. Thus, the court ordered William to pay 100% of the

1992-93 fees and a portion of the 1993-94 tuition. A hearing was ordered for arguments concerning William's obligation to pay the 1994-95 tuition.

College Expenses

Divorces often occur when the children of the marriage are quite young and college expenses are not as momentous as who gets the house, car or other tangible goods. Neglecting the issue of college costs in the divorce settlement, however, especially for the academically talented, is a serious mistake. As seen below, not addressing the issue properly can lead to protracted litigation.

In *McEntire v. Malloy* (1993), when the Malloys entered into their 1982 divorce agreement, the father agreed to pay $900.00 monthly child support per child and for the college education of the couple's daughter and son. Brooke, who was four years old at the time of the divorce, entered at age 12 into a special program for the academically gifted at Mary Baldwin College. The father began paying the $15,400.00 yearly cost toward the undergraduate degree and other miscellaneous expenses, but ceased paying the $900.00 per month child support when Brooke entered Mary Baldwin College. The mother, who had custody of the children, sued for the past due support.

At issue was whether the obligation to pay child support continued while the father paid for Brooke's Mary Baldwin expenses. The father claimed that he told the mother that he would not simultaneously pay both college expenses and child support and that an oral contract existed between the parents to cease support payments when a child entered college. Obviously, neither parent anticipated that Brooke would enter college at age 12 and be on schedule to receive her B.A. degree at age 16.

Although the mother argued no such oral contract existed and Brooke spent summers and holidays at home and thus support was warranted for the residential periods, the Arkansas chancellor (judge) found there was an oral contract to modify the support agreement. Because the father relied in good faith upon the oral contract, the doctrine of *equitable estoppel* (one is precluded from receiving a benefit through one's own action) prevented the mother's collection of the delinquent child support. The Arkansas Court of Appeals refused to disturb the chancellor's decision, stating the trial judge had the best opportunity to assess the credibility of the witnesses and his ruling was not against the preponderance of the evidence submitted at trial.

Another unusual college tuition case took place in New York when the parents of three highly gifted children omitted from their divorce agreement who should pay college costs. In *Shapiro v. Shapiro* (1982), the New York Supreme Court concluded that "special circumstances" required the father to pay the college expenses. Five criteria were used in the special circumstances test: (1) the educational background of the parents (in this case both had college degrees, and the mother had obtained a professional degree); (2) the environment in which the children were raised; (3) the expectations of the parents for their gifted children; (4) the children's superior academic abilities; and (5) the father's excellent financial status. The father argued unsuccessfully that a special circumstances test under New York law should be used only when support modifications were sought for "unanticipated" expenses. The trial judge disagreed, however, finding that the special circumstances analysis could be used not only to modify an agreement for unanticipated expenses, but also to increase an award for needs not covered in an original agreement.

An Iowa case, *Misol v. Misol* (1989), presents another interesting twist to the "who should pay" college expenses query when there is no clear answer in the dissolution agreement. Two of the four Misol children had entered college, and the father was paying $600.00 per month for child support, an obligation that existed under the decree until the children were age 18 or, under Iowa law, 22 years of age if the children were in college. As to the financial obligation for college, the father maintained that the children should pay since they held extensive funds in accounts under their own names. Unfortunately, there was no stated purpose for the existence of the accounts when they were created.

The trial court determined, and the Iowa Court of Appeals affirmed with one dissent, that the money in the children's accounts should be used to pay for their college expenses.

The record of the testimony of the father during the trial as to the intent in setting up these accounts evidently was convincing to a majority of the appellate court. The dissenting judge indicated that there was conflicting testimony in the record as to the purpose of the funds. There was a probability that at the time the gifts were made to the children the goal was to reduce parental tax liability, and that if the marriage had not dissolved, the parents would have supported the children through college and the use of the children's accounts would not have been an issue. Thus, the children were being penalized because of the parent's divorce. Instead of forcing the children to pay, the dissenting judge required the father to pay for two-thirds of the college expenses for an Iowa resident to attend a public university in Iowa, leaving to the children the choice of where to attend school.

Rohn v. Thuma (1980), described in *Gifted Children and the Law,* remains the best case illustrating the issue of the level of obligation of a parent paying for college. So important is that case that a brief summary bears repeating.

In the divorce decree, Edison Thuma agreed to pay the undergraduate college tuition, fees, and books of the couple's two children, provided he had the financial ability to do so, and the children had the mental ability and desire to attend college. Both children were academically gifted, and when the time came to attend college, one child chose to attend Vassar and the other child selected the University of Chicago, two universities with high tuition.

Thuma contended that the divorce decree required him to pay only the amount required for a "reasonable" college education and that by submitting the amount equal to the cost of attending a state university, he had complied with the decree. The trial court agreed and seemed to create the rule that whenever an obligation for higher education existed in a divorce settlement, the financial duty could be met by tendering the amount of the costs to attend a state university.

Fortunately for the interests of gifted children, the Indiana Court of Appeals reversed this broad brush approach. Instead of applying such a general rule, the appellate court concluded that the trial court must look at such matters as the ability of the paying parent to handle the outlay required for an expensive school, the advantages of a child to attend a high cost university, the child's mental ability, and the child's vocational goals. These guidelines make great sense when a court is looking at the college needs of a gifted child. A further plus for gifted students in the appeals court decision was the court's recommendation to counsel, in these types of cases, to try to assess children's educational needs, regardless of the age of the children at the time of the divorce, and attempt to predict the level of support that will be required to best serve the higher education needs of the children. It certainly makes sense to make such an effort, as it could save thousands of dollars in legal costs necessary to amend the original divorce settlement.

Child Custody

Historically, the two general doctrines that courts have applied in custody cases are the "tender years doctrine" and the "bests interests of the child." The tender years theory carried the presumption that custody of very young children should be awarded to the mother. Recently, this assumption has been under attack and so many states now have adopted more gender-neutral standards. The best interest approach remains viable, however, as states formulate, through their statute and court decisions, tests for deciding what is in the best interest of a child.

Regardless of the legislative and judicial mix in a state's custody jurisprudence, there will be a reference somewhere to the educational well-being of the child. In most instances, the educational consideration will be contained among several other general ones to be taken into account. How judges approach the educational well-being of a gifted child produces some interesting cases.

Available Education Opportunities

One such case is *Youngquist v. Kahle* (1995) where a Nebraska trial court initially awarded Richard and Cheryl Youngquist (now Kahle) joint custody of their three sons. But during a modification proceeding, the judge gave Richard sole custody of the children. After the 1990 divorce, both parties lived in Lincoln and the joint custody arrangement worked quite well. The difficulty arose when Cheryl's husband accepted employment in Big Springs, Nebraska, a town 300 miles from Lincoln. Cheryl filed a modification petition requesting that the court provide her sole custody so that she could move the boys to her new home. Richard objected on several grounds, one of which was that the two oldest boys were intellectually gifted and doing quite well in a local gifted education program.

At the modification hearing, the gifted education teacher testified that the two oldest children were "highly gifted" and presently had a mentor available to assist them. Testimony further indicated that the children probably would qualify for a program where during their high school years they could enroll in college courses at the University of Nebraska, Lincoln. Cheryl countered with the argument that Big Springs had an accelerated education program, but the trial judge concluded the Big Springs program did not appear to be equivalent to the gifted opportunities in Lincoln. While describing both Richard and Cheryl as fit parents, the trial judge found that a material change in circumstances had occurred and gave Richard sole custody of the children. Cheryl was ordered to pay $150.00 per month in child support, and a detailed visitation agreement was approved. Cheryl appealed to the Nebraska Court of Appeals.

Reaffirming the trial court judge's conclusion that the facts here made for a "tough decision," the appeals court found no abuse of discretion by the lower court. After examining relevant Nebraska statutory and case law, the appeals court found that the trial judge's concern for the continuity of the children's education and extracurricular activities supported the lower court's decision.

Like *Youngquist,* the Tennessee case *Goza v. Goza* (1993) concerned a custodial parent moving to a new location where the opportunity for gifted education was uncertain. At the dissolution of the marriage, the trial judge had awarded custody of then four-year-old daughter Tiffany to her mother, Crystal, with both parents signing an agreement that Tiffany would not be permanently moved from Tennessee without the approval of the court. Nine years later, Crystal requested a modification of the relocation prohibition, citing her current husband's opportunity for employment in Indianapolis.

The girl's father, Charles, objected to Tiffany leaving her hometown of Cleveland, Tennessee, arguing that his daughter had been identified as a gifted student and was participating in special programs for the gifted, including enrollment in a gifted student program at a local university. Basing his decision on this information and on evidence that Tiffany was successfully participating in athletic programs and had ties to other family members in the area, the trial judge awarded sole custody to Charles. Crystal appealed the change of custody decision to the state court of appeals.

The appeals court affirmed the trial judge's change of custody. As in *Youngquist,* the appellate panel concurred that the custody decision was a difficult choice. Both parents had remarried, both were attentive to Tiffany's well-being, and Crystal's current husband had tried to find employment in the Cleveland area so that Tiffany could remain there. Although

Crystal had investigated the gifted educational opportunities for Tiffany in Indianapolis, the appeals court pointed out that the local college gifted program was a "known quantity and one in which Tiffany is already established." These gifted education concerns, family ties, and local athletic opportunities resulted in the appeals court agreeing with the trial court that it was in Tiffany's best interest to remain in Cleveland with her father.

Enhanced Educational Opportunities

Three cases touch upon the issue of modifying custody to move a child to a location where greater resources for the child would be available. All three petitioners lost, probably because the benefit of the change of residence to the child was somewhat vague. In *Carpenter v. Carpenter* (1979), the mother, who had custody of the children and lived in Virginia, could not find employment as a chemist in the Tidewater area. She wished to move to New York City to seek employment, and she also claimed that her gifted children would enjoy greater educational and cultural advantages in New York. The father, who lived in Norfolk and had a close relationship with the seven-and nine-year-old children, was granted a permanent injunction by the trial court to prevent the children from being moved from Virginia without the court's permission. On appeal, the appellate judges examined the factors that the trial judge used to determine whether the best interests of the children were served by staying in Virginia, including the finding that the cultural and educational advantages in New York were not significantly greater than the cultural, educational and recreational advantages in Tidewater Virginia. The lower court's injunction was upheld.

Feather v. Feather (1998) is factually similar to *Carpenter* and had the same outcome. At the time of the divorce litigation, three of the four Feather children (the youngest child was too young to be tested) had been identified as gifted with IQs in the "superior" range. This case, described as protracted by the Tennessee Court of Appeals, had numerous issues, but one of the important questions was whether the primary custodial parent, Dolly, could move the children from Nashville to Tucson. Morgan, the oldest son, had been admitted to a special program for gifted students at the University of Arizona, and Dolly pointed out to the court that the Tucson school district had seventeen Advanced Placement courses compared to only two such opportunities at the local county school. The trial judge denied Dolly's request for the move, and the issue became one of five major issues before the Tennessee appellate court.

Speaking about the relocation issue, the appellate opinion cited the trial court's findings that there was "proof that the Tennessee school system is adequate for these children" and that the plan to move to Arizona was primarily motivated to undermine the father's relationship with the children. Therefore, the appeals court held that the lower court's denial of the relocation petition should stand.

Stable Education Environment

Dickison v. Dickison (1994) involved a change of custody for a gifted child with a record of behavioral problems. The child, M.B.D., lived with his mother, Sandra, in Topeka, Kansas, but spent time with his father who lived in the Kansas City suburb of Overland Park, Kansas. The father, Roscoe, petitioned the trial court for a change in custody, claiming that M.B.D.'s increasing behavioral problems constituted a material change of circumstances sufficient to support the alteration. M.B.D.'s behavioral problems were considerable, involving psychiatric treatment, stays in residential treatment centers, and an appointment of a guardian. Roscoe believed that much of M.B.D.'s behavioral difficulty was related to his being gifted. He was a teacher of the gifted in the Kansas City, Missouri school system, a board member of Shawnee Mission Association of the Gifted, and a resident of the culturally and educationally nourishing Kansas City community, and believed that he could serve M.B.D.'s needs better than Sandra. Interestingly, the trial judge did not find that Roscoe met the burden of proof for a material change of circumstances ruling, but on *sua sponte* (the court's own initiative), ordered M.B.D. to reside with Roscoe. After an unsuccessful hearing to alter or amend the trial court's decision, Sandra appealed the case to the Kansas Court of Appeals.

The appellate court affirmed the lower court by finding that the district court did not abuse its discretion in awarding custody to Roscoe. While Roscoe's claims did not meet the requirements to constitute a material change in circumstances, the appellate court concluded that the testimony presented at the initial proceeding and at the subsequent hearing to amend the *sua sponte* ruling were sufficient to support the trial judge's decision order a change of custody.

A stable living environment was also the concern in the 1995 Georgia case, *Villenueve v. Richbourg (1995)*. Maria Villenueve petitioned for custody of her minor child, Brandin, whose custody at the dissolution of her marriage to Christopher Allen had been awarded to the paternal great-grandmother, Mary Richbourg. The child was 16 months old at the time of the 1984 divorce, and Maria and Christopher were still in their teens. Maria was not found to have been an unfit parent at the time of the divorce, but after examining the facts of the case, the trial court awarded permanent custody to the great-grandmother.

A decade later, Maria, now remarried and working as a nurse, requested that Brandin be returned to her. The trial court, however, stated that Maria had to show with clear and convincing evidence that she was a fit parent and that it was in the best interest of the child to change custody. It was the best interest standard that Maria could not meet. The trial court found that the now 77-year-old Mary had provided the child a stable home. The child was enrolled in a gifted academic program, the father and the maternal grandmother who lived in the community aided Brandin, and the child had no behavioral problems. A Georgia appellate court concluded there was no abuse of discretion by the trial judge in leaving Brandin in this stable environment.

Custody and School Choice

Goldman v. Logue (1984), described in Chapter Five in *Gifted Education and the Law (Karnes & Marquardt,* 1991), concerned a mother's unsuccessful attempt to obtain a change of custody so that a child could be switched from a public to a private school. *Lombardo v. Lombardo* (1993) concerned a mother's attempt to secure a court order to have her child attend a gifted program.

During their divorce proceeding, Maureen and Charles Lombardo were awarded joint custody of their three sons, Michael, Robert, and Erin, with Charles having primary physical custody of all three children. Maureen petitioned the trial court to order that Robert, who ranked fourth out of 900 students on the third-grade placement test, be admitted to the school district's talented and gifted program. Charles, basing his decision on Michael's participation in the program, thought Robert would be a more well-rounded student if he did not participate. Since Charles was the primary custody parent, the trial court stated that his decision should control.

The Michigan Court of Appeals vacated the decision and remanded the case to the lower court. The appellate court stated that, in joint custody arrangements when a significant decision such as education is to be made concerning the child, the standard for decision-making should be based on the best interest of the child, not on which parent has physical custody. The trial court could hear evidence as to what curriculum would be best for Robert.

Summary

Generalizations are difficult to make in these domestic relations cases. One general conclusion is that judges appear sensitive to the well-being of the intellectually gifted child, even more so than some other segments of the population who view the gifted child unsympathetically or, in some instances, with clear hostility. Perhaps the experiences of having a legal education and working with professionally trained people on a daily basis make judges more appreciative of, and sensitive to, intellectual ability.

The above cases also send signals to attorneys and parents about how to avoid potential difficulties that arise when a gifted child is involved in a domestic relations matter. For example, if money is to be set aside for the college education of children, this purpose should be recorded at the time of the creation of the account. Even if a child is in grade school at the time of the divorce, college costs should be predicted as accurately as possible, lest one parent be thinking of a community college while the other is thinking of Princeton. In addition, parents should remember that many states require support payments to continue through age twenty-one or twenty-two, after the child is in college. This results in the overlapping of support payments with the expenditure for college tuition, fees, and books.

Finally, the cases illustrate that imprecise claims for increased child support or alteration of the custody arrangements seldom work. Instead, parents must show specific benefits to the court, such as a new school's more extensive curriculum, higher test scores of students enrolled, opportunities for individualized instruction, and other such benefits. In custody cases, vague arguments, such as the new city is larger or culturally more sophisticated, are not going to persuade a judge who probably has strong ties to the local community. State statutes, regulations, and judicial guidelines often contain ambiguous language relating to the educational needs of children, leaving trial judges considerable discretion. Claims supported by detailed evidence lessen the chance that the interests of a gifted child will be injured by an erroneous decision.

References

Karnes, F.A. and Marquardt, R.G. (1991). *Gifted children and the law: Mediation, due process, and court cases.* Scottsdale, AZ: Gifted Psychology Press (formerly Ohio Psychology Press).

Krementz, J. (Ed.). (1989). *How it feels to fight for your life.* Boston: Little, Brown & Company.

Court Cases

Addy v. Addy, 456 N.W.2d 506 (N.D. 1990).

Carpenter v. Carpenter, 257 S.E.2d 845 (Va. 1979).

Dickison v. Dickison, 874 P.2d 695 (Kan. Ct. App. 1994).

District of Columbia v. Howell, 607 A.2d 501 (D.C. App. 1992).

Feather v. Feather, No. 13,840, 1998 LEXIS 233 (Tenn. Ct. App. Apr. 3, 1998).

Goldman v. Logue, 461 So.2d 469 (La. App. 5th Cir. 1984).

Goza v. Goza, No. 03a01-9306-GS-00213, 1993 LEXIS 702 (Tenn. Ct. App. Nov. 15, 1993).

Hoefers v. Jones, 672 A.2d 1299 (N. J. Super. Ch. Div. 1994).

Howard v. Howard, 301 So.2d 191 (Ala. 1974).

Lombardo v. Lombardo, 507 N.W.2d 788 (Mich. Ct. App. 1993).

McEntire v. Malloy, No. CA 92-992, 1993 LEXIS 239 (Ark. Ct. App. Apr. 21, 1993).

Misol v. Misol, 445 N.W.2d 411 (Iowa Ct. App. 1989).

Moore v. Tucson Elec. Power Co., 761 P. 2d 1091 (Ariz. Ct. App. 1988).

O'Campo v. The School Board Of Dade County, 589 So. 2d 323 (Fla. District Ct. App. 1991).

Rohn v. Thuma, 408 N.E.2d 578 (Ind. App. 1980).

Scott v. Scott, No. 88-156-II, 1988 LEXIS 668 (Tenn. Ct. App. Nov. 2, 1988).

Shapiro v. Shapiro, 455 N.Y.S.2d 157 (N.Y. Sup. Ct. 1982).

Umstot vs Umstot, 968 S.W. 2d 819 (Tenn. App. 1997).

Villenueve v. Richbourg, 457 S.E.2d 821 (Ga. Ct. App. 1995).

Youngquist v. Kahle, 531 N.W.2d 260 (Neb. Ct. App. 1995).

9

Gifted Children and the Office for Civil Rights

The Office for Civil Rights (OCR) in the U.S. Department of Education (DE) is designated to enforce five federal civil rights laws prohibiting discrimination on the basis of race, color, national origin, sex, disability, and age in activities and programs receiving federal assistance. The federal civil rights laws are:

- Title VI of the Civil Rights Act of 1964, which prohibits discrimination on the basis of race, color, or national origin;
- Title IX of the Education Amendments of 1972, which prohibits discrimination on the basis of sex in educational programs;
- Section 504 of the Rehabilitation Act of 1973, which prohibits discrimination on the basis of physical and mental disability;
- The Age Discrimination Act of 1975, which prohibits discrimination on the basis of age; and
- Title II of the Americans with Disabilities Act of 1990, which prohibits discrimination on the basis of disability.

The overall mission of OCR is to ensure equal access to education and promote educational excellence across the nation through vigorous enforcement of civil rights. Resolving complaints is a primary responsibility. OCR provides support to other DE programs as well. It also provides technical assistance to help institutions achieve voluntary compliance of the civil rights laws enforced by the OCR. Compliance reviews are agency initiated cases that permit OCR to target resources where compliance problems appear particularly acute.

All state educational agencies, elementary and secondary school districts, colleges and universities, vocational schools, proprietary schools, state rehabilitation agencies, libraries, and museums receiving U.S. Department of Education funds must be in compliance. Admissions, recruitment, financial aid, academic programs, student treatment and services, counseling and guidance, discipline, classroom assignments, grading, vocational education, recreation, physical education, athletics, housing, and employment may be included. Additionally, certain grant programs are also a focus of OCR.

OCR consists of administrative offices located in the U.S. Department of Education in Washington, D.C. with the staff providing legal, policy, and management support. There are twelve enforcement offices. A listing is provided at the end of this chapter. Individuals in the enforcement offices resolve complaints and conduct compliance reviews. They also conduct a comprehensive program of technical assistance. Karnes and Marquardt (1994) identified the major responsibilities of OCR which include investigating complaints filed by an individual or representative who believes he/she has been discriminated against. In addition, OCR may initiate compliance reviews and monitor the progress of eliminating discriminatory practices in institutions and agencies implementing plans negotiated by them. Negotiation is the method employed to resolve complaints. However, if unable to do so, OCR will bring the actions necessary to enforce the aforementioned five laws. Technical assistance is provided to help institutions achieve voluntary compliance with OCR. In addition, OCR provides services to other U.S. Department of Education programs.

A Complaint

Anyone may file a complaint who believes that an educational institution that receives federal money has discriminated against someone on the basis of race, color, national origin, disability, sex, or age. The person or organization filing the complaint may not be the victim of the alleged discrimination, but may file on behalf of another individual or group.

To file a formal complaint, one may seek the Discrimination Complaint Form from the nearest OCR or send name/address along with business hours phone number. This information should contain a general description of the person(s) or class of people injured by the alleged discrimination although names are not required. Also included should be the name and address of the institution (school) that committed the alleged discrimination. All of this information should be followed by a description in sufficient detail to assist OCR to understand what occurred, when it happened, and the basis for the alleged discrimination. A complaint must be filed within 180 days of the date of the alleged discrimination, unless the time line is extended by OCR.

Upon receipt of a complaint, the first priority of OCR is to resolve the allegations promptly and appropriately. The applicable law, policies, and procedures under which OCR may proceed to complaint resolution must be determined. A consent form will be forwarded and must be signed, dated, and returned within 30 calendar days or the complaint may be closed. The review usually takes another 30 days and notification of the decision will be given.

Karnes and Marquardt (1994) and Karnes, Troxclair,

and Marquardt (1997) have reported on the investigations conducted by OCR involving gifted students and their education. In each study the Freedom of Information Act (1966) was employed and the letters of findings requested. OCR agreed and eliminated all personally identifiable information from them. In the first cohort from 1985-1991, there were forty-eight letters of finding (Karnes and Marquardt, 1994). The second study of the OCR letters of findings from 1992-1995 revealed thirty-eight (Karnes, Troxclair, & Marquardt, 1997). There were a total of eighty-six letters of findings with the districts being in compliance fifty-two times. Of the total number, fifty-four pertained to African Americans. Hispanics, the disabled, limited English proficiency, Native Americans, East Indians, and a Caucasian followed in descending order. The major issues were admission to gifted programs, and the identification of gifted students. Others focused on staff assignments, IEP's, and the location of a fine arts program. It should be noted that most of the activity occurred in the southern states of Arkansas (10), Texas (9), South Carolina (6), Oklahoma (6), Virginia (5), and Georgia (5). California also had nine letters of findings.

    It appears that OCR is becoming a viable pathway for seeking solutions in gifted education for protected classes of students. Karnes and Marquardt (1994) noted that although a great number of districts have been found to be in compliance, there are benefits to OCR investigations. A series of communications take place between the district and OCR during the time the complaint is filed and the final letter of finding is issued. During this process, there is an opportunity for the district to alter policies in violation of regulations or to provide additional data indicating they are in compliance. This time period of negotiation is helpful to all parties as it allows flexibility in resolving the disputes. In addition, Karnes and Marquardt (1994) have noted the clarity and ease in reading the letters of findings as opposed to some due process reports and court cases.

It must be emphasized that there are not quotas or percentages of protected classes of students in gifted education set forth by OCR. Rather school districts must prove that their policies do not discriminate against these students. Some guidelines to take into consideration would be:

- Appoint a bi-racial committee to establish guidelines for screening and identification procedures which do not discriminate against minorities, disabled, female/male, and on the bases of age;
- Determine the eligibility criteria include multiple criteria for eligibility and multiple assessment measures; Inform all parents, students, and the community about the screening and identification procedures and the program(s);
- Provide staff development on an annual basis for all certified school personnel about the characteristics, nature and needs of all gifted and talented students;
- Utilize nondiscriminatory screening criteria and procedures which are directly related to the purpose of the gifted program;
- Ensure that all approved assessment instruments/measures are validated with respect to the population for whom they are being used; the instruments/measures accurately assess the abilities/skills intended to be measured; and the abilities/skills are consistent with the definition of the gifted used at the local/state level;
- Monitor by race, disability, gender, and age, the number of students nominated and identified in each individual school in the district to determine that discrimination does not occur;

- Initiate change, if and when needed, and
- Appoint a bi-racial appeals committee for the district.

The Office for Civil Rights has proven to be a viable vehicle for resolving discrimination on issues involving race, color, national origin, sex, disability and age in programs and activities receiving federal assistance. Karnes and Marquardt (1994) emphasized that complainants can delineate the issues, provide information, and discuss proposed solutions without worrying about technical court procedures. The underserved gifted must continue to be represented and protected, and this federal agency works to accomplish that goal.

References

Karnes, F. A. & Marquardt, R.G. (1994) Gifted education and discrimination: The role of the Office for Civil Rights. *Journal for the education of the gifted, 18*(1) 87-94.

Karnes, F.A., Troxclair, D.A. & Marquardt, R.G. (1997). The Office for Civil Rights and the gifted: An update. *Roeper Review, 19*(3) 162-163.

The Office for Civil Rights

U.S. Department of Education
Office for Civil Rights
Customer Service Team
Mary E. Switzer Building
330 C Street, SW
Washington, DC 20202
Telephone: (202) 205-5413; 1-800-421-3481
FAX: (202) 205-9862; TDD (202) 260-0471
Email: OCR@ED.Gov

Enforcement Offices

Eastern Division

Serving Connecticut, Maine, Massachusetts, New Hampshire, Rhode Island, Vermont

Office for Civil Rights, Boston Office
U.S. Department of Education
J. W. McCormack Post Office and Courthouse
Room 222, 01-0061
Boston, MA 02109-4557
(617) 223-9662; FAX (617) 223-9669;
TDD (617) 223-9695
Email: *OCR Boston@ed.gov*

Serving New Jersey, New York, Puerto Rico, Virgin Islands

Office for Civil Rights, New York Office
U.S. Department of Education
75 Park Place, 14th floor
New York, NY 10007-2146
(212) 637-6466; FAX (212)264-3803;
TDD (212) 637-0478
Email: *OCR NewYork@ed.gov*

Serving Delaware, Maryland, Kentucky, Pennsylvania, West Virginia

Office for Civil Rights, Philadelphia Office
U.S. Department of Education
Wanamaker Building, Suite 515
100 Penn Square East
Philadelphia, PA 19107
(215) 656-8541; FAX (215) 656-8605;
TDD (215) 656-8604
Email: *OCR Philadelphia@ed.gov*

Southern Division

Serving Alabama, Florida, Georgia, South Carolina, Tennessee

Office for Civil Rights, Atlanta Office
U.S. Department of Education
61 Forsyth St. S.W., Suite 19T70
Atlanta, GA 30303-3104
(404) 562-6350; FAX (404) 562-6455;
TDD (404) 331-7236
Email: *OCR Atlanta@ed.gov*

Serving Arkansas, Louisiana, Mississippi, Oklahoma, Texas

Office for Civil Rights, Dallas Office
U. S. Department of Education
1999 Bryan Street, Suite 2600
Dallas, TX 75201
(214) 880-2459; FAX (214) 880-3082;
TDD (214) 880-2456
Email: *OCR Dallas@ed.gov*

Serving North Carolina, Virginia, Washington, DC

Office for Civil Rights, District of Columbia Office
U.S. Department of Education
1100 PA. Ave, N.W., Rm. 316
P.O. Box 14620
Washington D.C. 20044-4620
(202) 208-2545; FAX (202) 208-7797;
TDD (202) 208-7741
Email: *OCR@ed.gov*

Midwestern Division

Serving Illinois, Indiana, Minnesota, Wisconsin

Office for Civil Rights, Chicago Office
U.S. Department of Education
111 N. Canal Street Suite 1053
Chicago, IL 60606-7204
(312) 886-8434; FAX (312)353-4888;
TDD (312)353-2540
Email: *OCR Chicago@ed.gov*

Serving Michigan & Ohio

Office for Civil Rights, Cleveland Office
U.S. Department of Education
600 Superior Avenue East
Bank One Center, Room 750
Cleveland, OH 44114-2611
(216) 522-4970; FAX (216) 522-2573;
TDD (216) 522-4944
Email: *OCR Cleveland@ed.gov*

Serving Iowa, Kansas, Missouri, Nebraska, North Dakota, South Dakota

Office for Civil Rights, Kansas City Office
U.S. Department of Education
10220 North Executive Hills Boulevard
8th floor, 07-6010
Kansas City, MO 64153-1367
(816) 880-4200; FAX (816) 891-0644;
TDD (816) 891-0582
Email: *OCR KansasCity@ed.gov*

Western Division

Serving Arizona, Colorado, Montana, New Mexico, Utah, Wyoming

Office for Civil Rights, Denver Office
U.S. Department of Education
Federal Building, Suite 310, 08-7010
1244 Speer Boulevard
Denver, CO 80204-3582
(303) 844-5695; FAX (303) 844-4303;
TDD (303) 844-3417
Email: *OCR Denver@ed.gov*

Serving California

Office for Civil Rights, San Francisco Office
U.S. Department of Education
Old Federal Building, 09-8010
50 United Nations Plaza, Room 239
San Francisco, CA 94102-4102
(415) 437-7700; FAX (415) 437-7783;
TDD (415) 437-7786
Email: *OCR SanFrancisco@ed.gov*

Serving Alaska, Hawaii, Idaho, Nevada, Oregon, Washington, American Samoa, Guam, Trust Territory of the Pacific Islands

Office for Civil Rights, Seattle Office
U.S. Department of Education
915 Second Avenue
Room 3310,10-9010
Seattle, WA 98174-1099
(206) 220-7900; FAX (206) 220-7887;
TDD (206) 220-7907
Email: *OCR Seattle@ed.gov*

10

Gifted Legal Issues in the New Millennium

What types of disputes involving gifted children are on the legal horizon? It is a safe bet that many of the types of issues discussed in the preceding chapters will continue to be the subject of mediation conferences, due process hearings, and court cases. Slowly, but surely, there is an evolving legal framework and body of law developing in this country that can be used to settle gifted education controversies.

In addition to the perennial disputes such as early admission, curriculum modification, teacher certification, nondiscriminatory testing, and the maintenance of racial diversity in programs, there likely will be new subject areas that will enter the legal resolution process. For example, as more children increasingly are home-schooled, some of these students may wish to take part in a public school's gifted education classes. At the time of this writing, no court case had been reported directly on this issue; selective participation by home-schooled children in other public school activities has reached the courts, however. These cases may have some predictive value that can be relied upon when similar cases involving gifted children are litigated.

In *Bradstreet v. Sobol* (1996), the parents of Jill Bradstreet, a child receiving home-schooling, requested that she be allowed to participate in interscholastic sports. The local superintendent in the New York school district rejected the requests, and the Bradstreets took their case to the courts. Among their claims was that since the superintendent had to approve the home school instruction program established for Jill, she was under New York law a "regularly enrolled" student and thus eligible to participate in the school district's athletic program. The parents also asserted that to deny participation would violate Jill's rights to due process and equal protection, rights protected by the state and federal constitutions.

None of the arguments was persuasive to a New York Supreme Court (in New York the supreme court is a trial court and the highest appellate court is the court of appeals). The court did not find home-schooling to be "regular enrollment" as defined by New York law. Nor did it find that the parents had the option of home-schooling or sending Jill to the public schools. If her parents wished Jill to participate in interscholastic sports, the solution was in their hands. Due process was not applicable, according to the court, because there was no fundamental right to participate in interscholastic athletics. Therefore, no due process had to be provided the Bradstreets. Finally, the court held that the equal protection argument was without merit as home-schooled children did not fall into the suspect class (defined in Chapter 2) category. Since the court found that the fundamental right and equal protections claims were not relevant, the applicable test was whether there was a rational basis for the state action banning participation. The court concluded that a sufficient rational basis in this case was the district's arguments that limiting participation to on-campus students would foster school loyalty, spirit, and create role models within the student body.

A second case might provide further insight into gifted home-schooled students' participation in public school activities. This case has the additional constitutional footing of religious freedom. This 1996 Oklahoma case, *Swanson v. Guthrie Independent School District No. 1,* introduced the federal constitution's First Amendment religious liberty protections into a dispute. Annie Swanson, who was being home-schooled, was given permission by the Guthrie superintendent to attend two one-hour seventh-grade classes. Before Annie's eighth grade year, the district changed superintendents and the new district head stated that Annie would have to obtain permission from the Guthrie Board of Education to be a part-time student in the eighth grade. When the Board denied the request, stating that the district could receive state funds only for full-time students, the Swanson case ended up in federal court.

The Swansons' arguments were that their daughter was being denied a free public education, they were being denied the constitutional right to direct the upbringing and education of their child, and that they were being denied their constitutional right to free exercise of religion as protected by the First Amendment of the federal constitution. The first two claims do not seem to have much substance. Their child could have a free public education, but it was the parents' choice to home school the child, a choice available to them under Oklahoma law. In addition, as discussed in Chapter 2, courts are frequently unwilling to create educational policy, and it would seem unlikely that a federal court would force the state of Oklahoma to create a right to a part-time education and also amend its financing practice of providing state aid to districts only for full-time students.

The free exercise argument, however, had some force and may have some relevance for future gifted education cases. According to the Swansons, they were educating Annie at home in order to foster their Christian beliefs. If their choices were limited by law to full-time or home-schooling with no option of part-time education, was this state-imposed policy placing a burden on their right to exercise their religious beliefs?

Unfortunately for the Swansons, the court found that two factors negated the free exercise of religion argument. First, they did not present to the court sufficient evidence to show how Annie's attendance at public school on a full-time basis burdened their religious freedom. Second, they did not show that their desire to send Annie to public school on a part-time basis furthered their religious beliefs. The federal court, therefore, held that the religious freedoms of the Swansons had not been infringed.

There was nothing in the court's opinion to indicate that Annie had been designated an intellectually gifted child, but there may be many gifted children who are today being home-schooled for religious reasons. Gifted/religious issues might become intertwined as parents seek public school services for their gifted, home-schooled children.

While again not a case involving a gifted child, a Massachusetts court was asked to rule on whether two visits per year by public school officials to the home of a child receiving home-schooling were a violation of the parents' religious freedom and their Fourth Amendment protection against unreasonable search and seizure (*Brunelle v. Lynn Public Schools*, 1997). Interestingly, when rejecting the constitutional arguments and upholding the school officials' visits, the court stated that periodic observation might be the only way to determine whether a student was competent or *gifted* (authors' italics) and that the home school plan enhanced the child's education.

Duran v. Nitche (1991) illustrates another way that gifted and constitutional issues can become entangled. Diana Duran was a student in an academically talented class. When asked to write a research paper on "The power of _____," Diana chose the topic, "The power of God." Included in her research plan was a survey of five questions that she wished teachers to administer to her fellow students. The survey asked the students whether they believed God had the power to control life and death and forgive sins. When the district refused to allow her teachers to administer the survey or to present her final report to the class (Diana would be allowed to present it to the teacher in the school library), the Durans sued the teacher, Linda Nitche, and the school board, claiming a violation of Diana's free speech rights under the First

Amendment and a violation of the equal protection clause of the Fourteenth Amendment.

A Pennsylvania federal court, however, did not support the Durans' arguments, deciding that there were several constitutional and pedagogical reasons for restricting Diana's report. Although noting that constitutional rights do not end at the schoolhouse door, the court held that the school had the right to regulate speech content in the classroom. A classroom, the court pointed out, is not a traditional public forum such as a street corner or public park where free speech has significant constitutional protection, unless the school takes action to make it a public arena. In addition, the court considered the maturity of the children, the view that the teacher's participation in the survey and the classroom report might seem an endorsement of religion, a violation of the First Amendment's establishment clause that prohibits states from endorsing a specific religious belief. Finding no First Amendment violation, the court upheld the school district's restrictions as rationally related to the district's educational mission. The equal protection argument likewise was not persuasive as the court pointed out that Diana failed to present evidence showing that she was being discriminated against as a member of a suspect class.

A third type of constitutional issue, based on economic status and race, was the subject of a recent American Civil Liberties Union (ACLU) suit filed against the Inglewood (California) school district (*Bias Suit,* 1999). The suit claimed that the school district did not offer Advanced Placement Program (AP) classes in lower socioeconomic schools, thus, discriminating against poor Latino and black students. The ACLU is currently representing four students with the intent of forcing the school district and the State Department of Education to be sensitive to the intellectual needs of all students. This is an innovative suit, and given the breadth of ACLU offices around the country and its interest in the welfare of children and ending discrimination, one that could have implications for gifted education policy.

Whether future disputes stem from the more traditional gifted education issues or from newly identified controversies, it is essential that the matters be settled in ways that foster children's educational development. It is a truism that individual productivity is a key to America's success in the fields of education, government, the arts, technology, medical care, and economics. Not providing appropriate educational services to gifted and talented children is extremely detrimental to America as it competes with other nations. Most importantly, this is injurious to the intellectual well-being of one of our country's greatest resources—its gifted children. To develop their potential, however, it is necessary that the special needs of gifted children be explicitly recognized though legal means, whether in statutes, court cases, or administrative rulings.

References

Sahagun, L., & Weiss, K. (1999, July 28). Bias suit targets schools without advanced classes. *Los Angeles Times*, p.A1.

Court Cases

Bradstreet v. Sobol, 650 N.Y.S.2d 402 (N.Y. App. Div. 1996).

Brunelle v. Lynn Public School, No. 95-1312 A 1997 LEXIS 73 (Mass. Sup. Ct. Dec. 17, 1997).

Duran v. Nitsche, 780 F. Supp. 1048 (E.D. Pa. 1991).

Swanson v. Guthrie School District No. 1, 942 F. Supp. 511 (W.D. Okla. 1996).

Jacob K. Javits Gifted and Talented Students Education Act of 1988

TITLE 20 — Education
CHAPTER 70 — Strengthening and Improvement of Elementary and Secondary Schools
SUBCHAPTER X — Programs of National Significance
Part B — Gifted and Talented Children

Sec. 8032. Jacob K. Javits Gifted and Talented Students Education Act

(a) Findings and purposes

The Congress finds and declares that—

(1) all students can learn to high standards and must develop their talents and realize their potential if the United States is to prosper;

(2) gifted and talented students are a national resource vital to the future of the Nation and its security and well-being;

(3) too often schools fail to challenge

students to do their best work, and students who are not challenged will not learn to challenging State content standards and challenging State student performance standards, fully develop their talents, and realize their potential;

(4) unless the special abilities of gifted and talented students are recognized and developed during such students' elementary and secondary school years, much of such students' special potential for contributing to the national interest is likely to be lost;

(5) gifted and talented students from economically disadvantaged families and areas, and students of limited-English proficiency are at greatest risk of being unrecognized and of not being provided adequate or appropriate educational services;

(6) State and local educational agencies and private nonprofit schools often lack the necessary specialized resources to plan and implement effective programs for the early identification of gifted and talented students and for the provision of educational services and programs appropriate to their special needs;

(7) the Federal Government can best carry out the limited but essential role of stimulating research and development and personnel training and providing a national focal point of information and technical assistance that is necessary to ensure that the Nation's schools are able to meet the special educational needs of gifted and talented students, and thereby serve a profound national interest; and

(8) the experience and knowledge gained

in developing and implementing programs for gifted and talented students can and should be used as a basis to—

(A) develop a rich and challenging curriculum for all students; and

(B) provide all students with important and challenging subject matter to study and encourage the habits of hard work.

(b) Statement of purpose

It is the purpose of this part—

(1) to provide financial assistance to State and local educational agencies, institutions of higher education, and other public and private agencies and organizations, to initiate a coordinated program of research, demonstration projects, personnel training, and similar activities designed to build a nationwide capability in elementary and secondary schools to meet the special educational needs of gifted and talented students;

(2) to encourage the development of rich and challenging curricula for all students through the appropriate application and adaptation of materials and instructional methods developed under this part; and

(3) to supplement and make more effective the expenditure of State and local funds, for the education of gifted and talented students.

(Public L. 89-10, title X, Sec. 10202, as added Public L. 103-382, title I, Sec. 101, Oct. 20, 1994, 108 Stat. 3820.)

Sec. 8033 Construction

Nothing in this part shall be construed to prohibit a recipient of funds under this part from serving gifted and talented students simultaneously with students with similar educational needs, in the same educational settings where appropriate.

(Public L. 89-10, title X, Sec. 10203, as added Public L. 103-382, title I, Sec. 101. Oct. 20, 1994, 108 Stat. 3822.)

Sec. 8034. Authorized programs

(a) Establishment of program

(1) In general

From the sums appropriated under section 8037 of this title in any fiscal year the Secretary (after consultation with experts in the field of the education of gifted and talented students) shall make grants to or enter into contracts with State educational agencies, local educational agencies, institutions of higher education, or other public agencies and private agencies and organizations (including Indian tribes and Indian organizations (as such terms are defined by the Indian Self-Determination and Education Assistance Act [25 U.S.C. 450 et seq.]) and Native Hawaiian organizations) to assist such agencies, institutions, and organizations which submit applications in carrying out programs or projects authorized by this part that are designed to meet the educational needs of gifted and talented students, including the training of personnel in the education of gifted and talented students and in the use, where appropriate, of gifted and talented services, materials, and methods for all students.

(2) Application

Each entity desiring assistance under this part shall submit an application to the Secretary at such time, in such manner, and containing such information as the Secretary may reasonably require. Each such application shall describe how—

(A) the proposed gifted and talented services, materials, and methods can be adapted, if appropriate, for use by all students; and
(B) the proposed programs can be evaluated.

(b) Uses of funds

Programs and projects assisted under this section may include—

(1) professional development (including fellowships) for personnel (including leadership personnel) involved in the education of gifted and talented students;

(2) establishment and operation of model projects and exemplary programs for serving gifted and talented students, including innovative methods for identifying and educating students who may not be served by traditional gifted and talented programs, summer programs, mentoring programs, service learning programs, and cooperative programs involving business, industry, and education;

(3) training of personnel and parents involved in gifted and talented programs with respect to the impact of gender role socialization on the educational needs of gifted and talented children and in gender equitable education methods, techniques and practices;

(4) implementing innovative strategies, such as cooperative learning, peer tutoring and service learning;

(5) strengthening the capability of State educational agencies and instructions of higher education to provide leadership and assistance to local educational agencies and nonprofit private schools in the planning, operation, and improvement of programs for the identification and education of gifted and talented students and the appropriate use of gifted and talented programs and methods to serve all students;

(6) programs of technical assistance and information dissemination, including how gifted and talented programs and methods, where appropriate, may be adapted for use by all students; and

(7) carrying out:

(A) research on methods and techniques for identifying and teaching gifted and talented students, and for using gifted and talented programs and methods to serve all students; and

(B) program evaluations, surveys, and the collection, analysis, and development of information needed to accomplish the purposes of this part.

(c) Establishment of National Center

(1) In general

The Secretary (after consultation with experts in the field of the education of gifted and talented students) shall establish a National Center for Research and Development in the Education of Gifted and Talented Children and Youth through grants to or contracts with one or more institutions of higher education or State educational agency, or a combination or consortium of such institutions and agencies, for the purpose of carrying out activities described in paragraph (7) of subsection (b) of this section.

(2) Director

Such National Center shall have a Director. The Secretary may authorize the Director to carry out such functions of the National Center as may be agreed upon through arrangements with other institutions of higher education, State or local educational agencies, or other public or private agencies and organizations.

(d) Limitation

Not more than 30 percent of the funds available in any fiscal year to carry out the programs and projects authorized by this section may be used to conduct activities pursuant to subsection (b) (7) or (c) of this section.

(e) Coordination

Research activities supported under this section—
(1) shall be carried out in consultation with the Office of Educational Research and Improvement to ensure that such activities are coordinated with and enhance the research and development activities supported by such Office; and
(2) may include collaborative research activities which are jointly funded and carried out with such Office.

(Public L. 89-10, title X, Sec. 10204, as added Public L. 103-382, title I, Sec. 101, Oct. 20, 1994, 108 Stat. 3822.)

References in Text

The Indian Self-Determination and Education Assistance Act, referred to in subsec. (a) (1), is Public L. 93-638, Jan. 4, 1975, 88 Stat. 2203, as amended, which is classified principally to subchapter II (Sec. 450 et seq.) of chapter 14 of Title 25, Indians. For complete classification of this Act to the Code, see Short Title note set out under section 450 of Title 25 and Tables.

Section Referred to in Other Sections

This section is referred to in section 8035 of this title.

Sec. 8035. Program priorities

(a) General priority

In the administration of this part the Secretary shall give highest priority—
(1) to the identification of and the provision of services to gifted and talented students who may not be

identified and served through traditional assessment methods (including economically disadvantaged individuals, individuals of limited-English proficiency, and individuals with disabilities); and

(2) to programs and projects designed to develop or improve the capability of schools in an entire State or region of the Nation through cooperative efforts and participation of State and local educational agencies, institutions of higher education, and other public and private agencies and organizations (including business, industry, and labor), to plan, conduct, and improve programs for the identification of and service to gifted and talented students, such as mentoring and apprenticeship programs.

(b) Service priority

In approving applications for assistance under section 8034 (a) (2) of this title, the Secretary shall assure that in each fiscal year at least one-half of the applications approved under such section address the priority described in subsection (a) (1) of this section.

(Public L. 89-10, title X, Sec. 10205, as added Public L. 103-382, title I, Sec. 101, Oct. 20, 1994, 108 Stat. 3823.)

Sec. 8036. General provisions

(a) Participation of private school children and teachers

In making grants and entering into contracts under this part, the Secretary shall ensure, where appropriate, that provision is made for the equitable participation of students and teachers in private nonprofit elementary and secondary schools, including the participation of teachers and other personnel in professional development programs serving such children.

(b) Review, dissemination, and evaluation

The Secretary shall—

(1) use a peer review process in reviewing applications under this part;

(2) ensure that information on the activities and results of programs and projects funded under this part is disseminated to appropriate State and local agencies and other appropriate organizations, including nonprofit private organizations; and

(3) evaluate the effectiveness of programs under this part in accordance with section 8941 of this title, both in terms of the impact on students traditionally served in separate gifted and talented programs and on other students, and submit the results of such evaluation to Congress not later than January 1, 1998.

(c) Program operations

The Secretary shall ensure that the programs under this part are administered within the Department by a person who has recognized professional qualifications and experience in the field of the education of gifted and talented students and who shall—

(1) administer the programs authorized by this part;

(2) coordinate all programs for gifted and talented students administered by the Department;

(3) serve as a focal point of national leadership and information on the educational needs of gifted and talented students and the availability of educational services and programs designed to meet such needs; and

(4) assist the Assistant Secretary of the Office of Educational Research and Improvement in identifying research priorities which reflect the needs of gifted and talented students.

(Public L. 89-10, title X, Sec. 10206, as added Public L. 103-382, title I, Sec. 101, Oct. 20, 1994, 108 Stat. 3824.)

Sec. 8037. Authorization of appropriations

There are authorized to be appropriated $10,000,000 for fiscal year 1995 and such sums as may be necessary for each of the four succeeding fiscal years to carry out the provisions of this part.

(Public L. 89-10, title X, Sec. 10207, as added Public L. 103-382, title I, Sec. 101, Oct. 20, 1994, 108 Stat. 3824.)

Section Referred to in Other Sections

This section is referred to in section 8034
of this title.

B

Table of Cases

Addy v. Addy, 456 N.W.2d 506 (N.D. 1990).

Bennett v. New Rochelle School District, 497 N.Y.S. 2d 72 (1985).

Bradstreet v. Sobol, 650 N.Y.S.2d 402 (N.Y. App. Div. 1996).

Broadley v. Board of Education, 639 A.2d 502 (Conn. 1994).

Brownsville Area School District v. Student X, 729 A.2d 198 (Pa. Commw. Ct. 1999).

Brunelle v. Lynn Public School, No. 95-1312A, 1997 LEXIS 73 (Mass. Sup. Ct. Dec. 17, 1997).

Carpenter v. Carpenter, 257 S.E.2d 845 (Va. 1979).

Centennial School District v. Commonwealth Board of Education, 539 A. 2d 785 (Pa. 1988).

Conrad Weiser Area School District v. Dept. of Education, 601 A.2d 701 (Pa. Commw. Ct. 1992).

Dallap v. Sharon City School District, 571 A.2d 368 (Pa. 1990).

Dickison v. Dickison, 874 P.2d 695 (Kan. Ct. App. 1994).

Dilley v. Slippery Rock Area School District, 625 A.2d 153 (Pa. Commw. 1993).

District of Columbia v. Howell, 607 A.2d 501 (D.C. App. 1992).

Duran v. Nitsche, 780 F. Supp. 1048 (E.D. Pa. 1991).

Egan v. Board of Education, 406 S.E. 2d 733 (W.Va. 1989).

Ellis v. Chester-Upland School District, 651 A.2d 616 (Pa. Commw. 1994).

Ex Parte Young, 209 U.S. 123 (1908).

Feather v. Feather, No. 13,840, 1998 LEXIS 233 (Tenn. Ct. App. Apr. 3, 1998).

Fowler v. Unified School District No. 259, 900 F. Supp. 1540 (D. Kan. 1995).

Goldman v. Logue, 461 So. 2d 469 (La. App. 5th Cir. 1984).

Goza v. Goza, No. 03a01-9306-GS-00123, 1993 LEXIS 702 (Tenn. Ct. App. Nov. 15, 1993).

Hoefers v. Jones, 672 A. 2d 1299 (N.J. Super. Ch. Div. 1994).

Hope v. Cortines, 69 F. 3d 687 (2nd Cir. 1995).

Howard v. Howard, 301 So.2d 191 (Ala. 1974).

Huldah A. v. Easton Area School District, 601 A. 2d. 860 (Pa. Commw. Ct. 1992).

Johnson v. Cassel, 387 S.E. 2d 553 (W. Va. 1989).

Keyes v. School District No. 1, 902 F. Supp. 1274 (D. Colo. 1995).

Lombardo v. Lombardo, 507 N.W.2d 788 (Mich. Ct. App. 1993).

Lorentzen v. Industrial Commission of Arizona, 790 P.2d 765 (Ariz. Ct. App. 1990).

McEntire v. Malloy, No. CA 92-992, 1993 LEXIS 239 (Ark. Ct. App. Apr. 21, 1993).

Misol v. Misol, 445 N.W.2d 411 (Iowa Ct. App. 1989).

Montana Board of Public Education v. Montana Admin. Code Com., Case No. BDV-91-1072 (unreported case).

Moore v. Tucson Electric Power Co., 761 P. 2d 1091 (Ariz. Ct. App. 1988).

New Brighton Area School District v. Matthew Z., 697 A.2d 1056 (Pa. Commw. 1997).

O'Campo v. The School Board of Dade County, 589 So. 2d 323 (Fla. District Ct. App. 1991).

Punxsutawney Area School District v. Dean, 663 A.2d 831 (Pa. Commw. Ct. 1995).

Punxsutawney Area School District v. Karouff is a companion case with *Dean* and can also be located at this citation.

Reynolds v. School District of Omaha, 461 N.W. 2d 758 (Neb. 1990).

Rohn v. Thuma, 408 N.E.2d 578 (Ind. App. 1980).

Rosenfeld v. Montgomery County Public School, 41 F. Supp. 2d 581 (D. Md. 1999).

Scott v. Scott, No. 88-156-II, 1988 LEXIS 668 (Tenn. Ct. App. Nov. 2, 1988).

Shapiro v. Shapiro, 455 N.Y.S.2d 157 (N.Y.Sup. Ct. 1982).

Simmons v. Board of Public Education, 843 F. Supp. 1296 (E.D. Ark. 1994).

Swanson v. Guthrie Independent School District No. 1, 942 F. Supp. 511 (W.D. Okla. 1996).

Umstot v. Umstot, 968 S.W. 2d 819 (Tenn. App. 1997).

Villenueve v. Richbourg, 457 S.E. 2d 821 (Ga. Ct. App. 1995).

West Virginia Board of Education v. Hechler, 376 S.E. 2d 839 (W.Va. 1988).

Wright v. Ector County Independent School District, 867 S.W. 2d 867 (Tex. App. Ct. 1993).

Youngquist v. Kahle, 531 N. W.2d 260 (Neb. Ct. App. 1995).

Zotos v. Lindbergh School District, 121 F. 3d 356 (8th Cir. 1997).

C

State Offices of Gifted Education

Listed below are the offices responsibile for the education of gifted children at the state level throughout the United States. These serve as an information resource concerning school services for gifted students in their respective state.

Alabama
Special Education Services
Alabama Department of Education
Gordon Persons Building
P.O. Box 302101
Montgomery, AL 36130-2101
(334) 242-8114
www.alsde.edu

Alaska
Gifted and Talented Education
Office of Special Education
Alaska Department of Education
801 West 10th Street, Suite 200
Juneau, AK 99801-1894
(907) 465-8691
www.educ.state.ak.us

Arizona
Arizona Department of Education
1535 West Jefferson Street
Phoenix, AZ 85007
(602) 542-3850
www.ade.state.az.us

Arkansas
Office of Gifted and Talented
Arkansas Department of Education
Room 103B, Education Building
4 State Capitol Mall
Little Rock, AR 72201
(501) 682-4224
http://ark.edu.k12.ar.us

California
Gifted and Talented Education
California Department of Education
P.O. Box 944272
Sacramento, CA 94244-2720
(916) 657-5257
www.goldmine.cde.ca.gov

Colorado
Gifted and Talented Education
Colorado Department of Education
201 East Colfax Avenue, Room 402
Denver, CO 80203
(303) 866-6849
www.cde.state.co.us

Connecticut
Gifted and Talented Programs
Connecticut Department of Education
25 Industrial Park Road
Middletown, CT 06457
(203) 638-4247
www.state.ct.us/sde

Delaware
Gifted and Talented Programs
Delaware Department of Public Instruction
P.O. Box 1402, Townsend Building
Dover, DE 19903-1402
(302) 739-4885
www.doe.state.de.us

District of Columbia
Gifted/Talented Education
District of Columbia Public Schools
Rabaut Administrative Building
N. Dakota & Kansas Aves., NW
Washington, DC 20011
(202) 576-6171

Florida
Bureau of Student Services/Exceptional Education
Florida Education Center, Suite 614
Tallahassee, FL 32399-0400
(904) 488-1106
www.firn.edu/doe

Georgia
Gifted Education/Curriculum Services
Georgia Department of Education
1870 Twin Towers East
Atlanta, GA 30334-5040
(404) 657-0182
www.doe.k12.ga.us

Hawaii
Student Support Services
Hawaii Department of Education
637 18th Avenue
Building C, #204
Honolulu, HI 96816
(808) 733-4476
www.k12.hi.us

Idaho
Special Education Services
Idaho State Department of Education
P.O. Box 83720
Boise, ID 83720-0027
(208) 332-6920
www.sde.state.id.us/dept

Illinois
Gifted and Talented Education
Illinois State Board of Education
100 North First Street
Springfield, IL 62777
(217) 782-3371
www.isbe.state.il.us

Indiana
Gifted/Talented Education Unit
Indiana Department of Education
Room 229, State House
Indianapolis, IN 46204-2798
(317) 232-9106
www.doe.state.in.us

Iowa
Gifted and Talented Education
Iowa Department of Education
Grimes State Office Building
Des Moines, IA 50319-0146
(515) 281-3199
www.state.ia.us/educate

Kansas
Gifted and Talented Education
Kansas State Board of Education
120 S.E. 10th Avenue
Topeka, KS 66612-1182
(785) 296-3857
www.ksbe.state.ks.us

Kentucky
Gifted and Talented Education
Kentucky Department of Education
Division of Professional Development
500 Mero Street, 17th Floor
Frankfort, KY 40601
(502) 564-2672
www.kde.state.ky.us

Louisiana
Gifted and Talented Program
Louisiana Department of Education
P.O. Box 94064
Baton Rouge, LA 70804-9064
(504) 763-3942
www.doe.state.la.us

Maine
Gifted and Talented Education
Maine Department of Education
State House Station #23
Augusta, ME 04333
(207) 287-5950
www.state.me.us/education/homepage.htm

Maryland
Student Achievement/Gifted and Talented Education
Maryland State Department of Education
200 West Baltimore Street
Baltimore, MD 21201-2595
(410) 767-0363
http://sailor.lib.md.us/msde

Massachusetts
Instructional and Curriculum Services
Massachusetts Department of Education
350 Main Street
Malden, MA 02148
(617) 388-3300. Ext. 260
http://info.doe.mass.edu

Michigan
Consultant for Talent Development
Curriculum Development Program
Michigan Department of Education
P.O. Box 30008
Lansing, MI 48909
(517) 373-4213
www.mde.state.mi.us

Minnesota
Office of Teaching and Learning
Children, Families and Learning Department
Minnesota Department of Education
624 Capitol Square Building
550 Cedar Street
St. Paul, MN 55101
(612) 297-7204
www.educ.state.mn.us

Mississippi
Gifted and Talented Programs
Mississippi Department of Education
Room 372, Office of Deputy Superintendent
P.O. Box 771
Jackson, MS 39205-0771
(601) 359-2588
http://mdek12.state.ms.us

Missouri
Gifted Education Programs
Missouri Department of Elementary and Secondary Education
P.O. Box 480
Jefferson City, MO 65102
(314) 751-2453
http://services.dese.state.mo.us

Montana
Gifted Education Services
Montana Office of Public Instruction
P.O. Box 202501
Helena, MT 59620-2501
(406) 444-4422
http://161.7.114.5/opi/opi.html

Nebraska
High-Ability Learner Education
Nebraska Department of Education
301 Centennial Mall South, Box 94987
Lincoln, NE 68509-4987
(402) 471-0737
www.nde.state.ne.us

Nevada
Gifted/Talented Education
Nevada Department of Education
700 East Fifth Street
Capitol Complex
Carson City, NV 89701
(702) 687-9141
www.nsn.k12.nv.us/nvdoe

New Hampshire
Office of Gifted Education
New Hampshire Department of Education
101 Pleasant Street
Concord, NH 03301
(603) 271-3769
www.state.nh.us/doe/education.html

New Jersey
Gifted and Talented Education
New Jersey Department of Education
100 Riverview, CN 500
Trenton, NJ 08625-0500
(609) 984-6308
www.state.nj.us/education

New Mexico
Special Education Department
New Mexico Department of Education
Education Building, Room 123
Santa Fe, NM 87501-2786
(505) 827-6508
www.sde.state.nm.us

New York
Summer Institutes
New York State Education Department
Room 981 EBA
Albany, NY 12234
(518) 474-8773
www.nysed.gov

North Carolina
Gifted Education Programs
State Department of Public Instruction
301 North Wilmington Street
Raleigh, NC 27601-2825
(919) 715-1999
www.dpi.state.nc.us

North Dakota
Curriculum Leadership and Improvement
Department of Public Instruction
State University Station Box 5036
Fargo, ND 58105-5036
(701) 231-6030
www.dpi.state.nd.us

Ohio
Division of Special Education
Ohio Department of Education
933 High Street
Worthington, OH 43085-4087
(614) 466-2650
www.ode.ohio.gov

Oklahoma
Gifted/Talented Education
Oklahoma Department of Education
2500 North Lincoln Boulevard
Oklahoma City, OK 73105-4599
(405) 521-4287
www.sde.state.ok.us

Oregon
Gifted/Talented Programs
Oregon Department of Education
255 Capitol Street, NE
Salem, OR 97310-0290
(503) 378-3598, ext 637
www.ode.state.or.us

Pennsylvania
Gifted Technical Assistance Program
Bureau of Special Education, 7th Floor
Pennsylvania Department of Education
333 Market Street
Harrisburg, PA 17126-0333
(717) 783-6913
www.cas.psu.edu/pde.html

Rhode Island
Gifted/Talented Programs
Rhode Island Department of Education
255 Westminster Street, Room 400
Providence, RI 02903-3400
(401) 277-4600 ext. 2318
http://instruct.ride.ri.net/ ride_home_page.html

South Carolina
Office of Technology Assistance
South Carolina Department of Education
803-A Rutledge Building
1429 Senate Street
Columbia, SC 29201
(803) 734-8335
www.state.sc.us/sde

South Dakota
Gifted Education
South Dakota Department of Education
700 Governors Drive
Pierre, SD 57501-2291
(605) 773-6400
www.state.sd.us/state/executive/deca

Tennessee
Gifted/Talented Programs
Tennessee Department of Education
710 James Robertson Parkway
8th Floor, Gateway Plaza
Nashville, TN 37243-0380
(615) 741-2851
www.state.tn.us/education

Texas
Gifted/Talented Education
Texas Education Agency
1701 North Congress Avenue
Austin, TX 78701
(512) 463-9455
www.tea.state.tx.us

Utah
Gifted and Talented Education
Utah State Office of Education
250 East 500 South
Salt Lake City, UT 84111
(801) 538-7743
www.usoe.k12.ut.us

Vermont
Gifted/Talented Education
Vermont Department of Education
120 State Street
Montpelier, VT 05620
(802) 828-3111
www.state.vt.us/educ

Virginia
Programs for the Gifted
Virginia Department of Education
P.O. Box 2120
Richmond, VA 23218-2120
(804) 371-7419
www.pen.k12.va.us

Washington
Gifted/Talented Education
Washington Office of Public Instruction
Old Capital Building
P.O. Box 47200
Olympia, WA 98504-7200
(360) 753-2858
www.ospi.wednet.edu

West Virginia
Office of Special Education
West Virginia Department of Education
Capitol Complex Building 6, Room 362
Charleston, WV 25305
(304) 558-0160
http://wvde.state.wv.us

Wisconsin
Gifted/Talented Education
Wisconsin Department of Public Instruction
125 South Webster Street
P.O. Box 7841
Madison, WI 53707-7841
(608) 266-3560
www.dpi.state.wi.us

Wyoming
Gifted/Talented Education
Wyoming Department of Education
Hathaway Building, 2nd Floor
2300 Capital Avenue
Cheyenne, WY 82002-0050
(307) 777-3544
www.k12.wy.us

State Associations for the Gifted

State Associations for the gifted are traditionally advocacy organizations for gifted students. Membership in these organizations includes parents, teachers, administrators, and researchers concerned with the education of gifted students. State associations lobby for legislation, provide information, sponsor annual conventions, and organize workshops. Listed below are the state associations that have current information.

Alabama Association for Gifted Children
665 Overland Road
Montevallo, AL 35115
(205) 620-1030

Arizona Association for the Gifted and Talented
P.O. Box 31088
Phoenix, AZ 85046-1088
(602) 482-8415
www.cap.ed.asu.edu/services/AAGT.html

Arkansans for Gifted and Talented Education
Ouachita Baptist University
Box 3702
Arkadelphia, AR 71998
(870) 245-5161

California Association for the Gifted
5777 W. Century Blvd., Suite 1670
Los Angeles, CA 90045
(310) 215-1898
www.CAGifted.org

Colorado Association for Gifted and Talented
P.O. Box 473414
Aurora, CO 80047-3414
(970) 353-0733

Connecticut Association for the Gifted
7 Mountain Spring Road
Farmington, CT 06032
(860) 677-1569

Delaware Talented and Gifted Association
P.O. Box 1402
Dover, DE 19903-1402
(302) 739-4885, ext. 3110

Florida Association for the Gifted
7740 NW 63rd Avenue
Parkland, FL 33067
(954) 341-3681
http://members.aol.com/pals222

Georgia Association for Gifted Children
890 F Atlanta Street, Suite 192
Roswell, GA 30075
(770) 645-5757
www.a-plus.net/GAGC

Hawaii Gifted Association
P.O. Box 22878
Honolulu, HI 96823-2878
(808) 732-1138

Idaho-The Association for Gifted
8325 Golse Drive
Boise, ID 83704
(208) 335-3511
http://coehp.idbsu.edu/itagsage

Illinois Association for Gifted Children
800 E. Northwest Hwy., Suite 610
Palantine, IL 60067
(847) 963-1892

Indiana Association for the Gifted
14436 US 24 West Roanoke
Indianapolis, IN 46783
(219) 672-3762

Presents of Mind Resource Show
Indiana Association for the Gifted
3923 Kitty Hawk Court
Carmel, IN 46033
(317) 844-3920

Iowa Talented and Gifted Association
206 6th Avenue, Suite 900
Des Moines, IA 50309-4018
(515) 282-8192
www.public.iastate.edu/~cbuxton/Itag/index.htm

Kansas Association for Gifted/Talented/Creative
P.O. Box 25281
Overland Park, KS 66225
(913) 681-4079
http://members.aol.com/cindys2449/KGTC.html

Kansas Parent Information Network
426 Olivette
McPherson, KS 67460
(316) 241-5654

Kentucky Association for Gifted Education
P.O. Box 9610
Bowling Green, KY 42102-9610
(502) 443-3098
www.montgomory.k12.ky.us/gifted-education/default.htm

Association for Gifted and Talented Students
Louisiana State University
228 Strauss Hall
Monroe, LA 71209
(318) 342-1275
http://kestner.chem.lsu.edu/lagt.htm

Maine Educators of the Gifted and Talented
3 Winding Way
Windham, ME 04062
(207) 236-4640

Maryland Coalition for Gifted and Talented
P.O. Box 3134
Crofton, MD 21114
(301) 598-5561

Massachusetts Association for Advancement of Individual Potential
Box 0065
Milton Village, MA 02187-0065
(617) 333-0223

Michigan Alliance for Gifted Education
P.O. Box 2237
Ann Arbor, MI 48106-2237
(313) 913-9913
www.geocities.com/EnchantedForest/1833/MAGEPAGE.HTM

Minnesota Council for the Gifted and Talented
5701 Normandale Rd.
Minneapolis, MN 55424
(612) 927-9546

Mississippi Association for Gifted Children
6241 Waterford
Jackson, MS 39211
(601) 898-8730

Gifted Association of Missouri
7507 NW Emerald Hills Drive
Kansas City, MO 64152
(816) 891-6488

Montana Association for Gifted and Talented Education, Inc.
3091 South Daffodil
Billings, MT 59102
www.wtp.net/~cabreras/agate.htm

Nebraska Association for the Gifted
ESU 16, 314 West 1st Street
Ogallala, NE 69153
(308) 284-8481
http://members.home.net/bbarbary

Nevada Association for Gifted and Talented
P.O. Box 60143
Las Vegas, NV 89160-0143
(702) 434-2165

New Hampshire Association for Gifted Education
P.O. Box 786
Hollis, NH 03049-0786
(603) 465-2012

The New Jersey Association for Gifted Children
P.O. Box 667
Mt. Laurel, NJ 08054
(609) 273-7530
http://home.att.net/~njagc/

Advocacy Association for Gifted and Talented Education
(AGATE) in New York State
Phoenicia Elementary School
P.O. Box 599
Phoenicia, NY 12464
(914) 688-5580
www.skidmore.edu/~tlam/ed/agate.htm

North Carolina Association for the Gifted and Talented
P.O. Box 899
Swansboro, NC 28584-0899
(910) 326-8463
http://198.85.168.187/organizations/page/ncagt.html

NC PAGE
16101 Henry Lane
Huntersville, NC 28078
(704) 875-0963

Ohio Association for Gifted Children
Lawrence County Education Service Center
Courthouse, 3rd Floor
Ironton, OH 45638
(740) 532-4223
www.oagc.com

Consortium of Ohio Coordinators for Gifted
Hamilton County Educational Service Center
11083 Hamilton Avenue
Cincinnati, OH 45231
(513) 742-2200, ext. 268

Oklahoma Association for Gifted, Creative and Talented
611 South Hoff Avenue
El Reno, OK 73036
(405) 262-3965

Network News Quarterly for Parents and Teachers of the Gifted
600 South College
Tulsa, OK 74104
(918) 631-5060

Oregon Association for Talented and Gifted
P.O. Box 1703
Beaverton, OR 97075
(503) 591-7899

Pennsylvania Association for Gifted Education
3026 Potshop Road
Norristown, PA 19403
(610) 584-5221
www.penngifted.org

Rhode Island State Advisory Committee on Gifted and Talented Education
150 Half Moon Trail
Wakefield, RI 02879
(410) 783-8052
www.ri.net/gifted_talented/rhode.html

South Carolina Consortium for Gifted Education
Lexington School District No. 1
P.O. Box 1869
Lexington, SC 29071
(803) 359-4178

South Dakota Association for Gifted Children
P.O. Box 757
Mitchell, SD 57301
(605) 996-3799

Tennessee Association for the Gifted
3059 Pittman Center Road
Sevierville, TN 37876
(423) 428-0538

Texas Association for the Gifted and Talented
406 East 11th, Suite 310
Austin, TX 78701-2617
(512) 499-8248
www-tenet.cc.utexas.edu/TAGT

Utah Association for Gifted Children
340 East 3545 South
Salt Lake City, UT 84115
(801) 461-9002

Vermont Network for the Gifted
University of Vermont
C-150 Living Learning Center
Burlington, VT 05405
(802) 985-3405

Virginia Association for the Gifted
Amherst County Public Schools
P.O. Box 1257
Amherst, VA 24521
(804) 946-9386
www.pen.k12.va.us/go/VAEG

Washington Association for Educators of the Talented and Gifted
4120 Point White Drive
Bainbridge Island, WA 98110
(360) 692-3101

Northwest Gifted Child Association
P.O. Box 1226
Bellevue, WA 98009
(425) 649-8546

West Virginia Gifted Education Association
George Washington High School
1522 Tennis Club Road
Charleston, WV 25314
(304) 348-7729
www.geocities.com/Athens/Olympus/4764/wvagt.html

Wisconsin Association for Talented and Gifted
1608 West Cloverdale Drive
Appleton, WI 54914
(920) 991-9177
www.uwgb.edu/~lorenzd

National Associations and Resources for the Gifted

American Association for Gifted Children
1121 West Main Street, Suite 100
Durham, NC 27701
(919) 683-1400
www.jayicom/sbi/aagc/index.html

ERIC Clearinghouse on Disabilities and Gifted Education
The Council for Exceptional Children
1920 Association Drive
Reston, VA 20191-1589
1-800-328-0272
www.cec.sped.org/ericec.htm

Gifted Child Society, Inc.
190 Rock Road
Glen Rock, NJ 07452
(201) 444-6530
www.gifted.org

Gifted Students Institute
Southern Methodist University
P.O. Box 750383
Dallas, TX 75275-0383
(214) 768-5437
www.smu.edu/~gsi/index.html

National Association for Gifted Children (NACG)
1707 L Street, NW
Suite 550
Washington, DC 20036
(202) 785-4268
www.nagc.org

National Research Center on the Gifted and Talented
The University of Connecticut
362 Fairfield Road, U-7
Storrs, CT 06269-2007
(203) 486-4826
www.ucc.uconn.edu/~wwwgt/nrcgt.html

National Talent Network
Education and Informational Resource Center (EIRC)
606 Delsea Drive
Sewell, NJ 08080
(609) 582-7000
www.eirc.org

Supporting Emotional Needs of the Gifted (SENG)
Kent State University
College of Education
405 White Hall
Kent, OH 44242
(330) 672-4450
www.educ.kent.edu/Frames/EFSS/SENG

World Council for Gifted and Talented Children, Inc.
18401 Hiawatha Street
Northridge, CA 91326
(818) 368-7501
www.worldgifted.org

Position Statements of the National Association for Gifted Children

Reprinted by permission of the
National Association for Gifted Children
1707 L Street, NW, Suite 550
Washington, DC 20036
202/785-4268
www.nagc.org

Position Statements

Beginning in 1991, the National Association for Gifted Children (NAGC) adopted a series of position papers to explain NAGC's position on topics of interest and controversy in education. Policy statements are designed to provide information on NAGC's views to interested colleagues in the field of education and the public at large.

Over time, members of the twenty-eight member Board of Directors drafted policy statements on given topics, some with the assistance of NAGC Divisions, which have been reviewed and discussed by the entire Board. After amendments and adjustments, statements that receive an 80 percent affirmative vote by Board members are considered to be the policy position of the organization. Currently there are 13 statements that have gone through this process.

Each of the 13 statements contains two initial paragraphs that explain the purpose of policy statements and place the statements in the context of NAGC's beliefs about general education. The introductory paragraphs are as follows:

> *The National Association for Gifted Children (NAGC) periodically issues policy statements dealing with issues, policies, and practices that have an impact on the education of gifted and talented students. Policy statements represent the official convictions of the organization.*
>
> *All policy statements approved by the NAGC Board of Directors are consistent with the organization's belief that education in a democracy must respect the uniqueness of all individuals, the broad range of cultural diversity present in our society, and the similarities and differences in learning characteristics that can be found within any group of students. NAGC is fully committed to national goals that advocate both excellence and equity for all students, and we believe that the best way to achieve these goals is through differentiated educational opportunities, resources, and encouragement for all students.*

For the purposes of this publication, a brief background statement has been added to each policy statement. As new issues arise, NAGC will continue to develop policy statements and standards of excellence for the field.

—**Sandra N. Kaplan**, President
—**James J. Gallagher**, Association Editor
October 1998

Appendix F–Position Statements of the National Association for Gifted Children

Ability Grouping

One of the time-honored methods used to adjust the educational program for gifted students has been to cluster them together in a single class or other identified groups, such as mathematics or reading. The goal of such grouping is to reduce the range of student abilities that must be addressed by the teacher. Ability grouping allows bright students to stimulate each other with ideas and challenge one another's thinking and problem-solving skills.

However, grouping students by ability has received mixed responses from educators. There is concern that such grouping will be unfair to those students who are not identified as part of specialized programs and who will not share in its advantages. Opposition becomes even more determined when grouping patterns reduce the cultural or ethnic diversity of the classes. As a result, ability grouping is one of the most controversial issues in the education of gifted children. Many different versions of grouping have been tried to ensure both equity and excellence result from this program adaptation.

Ability Grouping Position Statement

The National Association for Gifted Children (NAGC) periodically issues policy statements dealing with issues, policies, and practices that have an impact on the education of gifted and talented students. Policy statements represent the official convictions of the organization.

All policy statements approved by the NAGC Board of Directors are consistent with the organization's belief that education in a democracy must respect the uniqueness of all individuals, the broad range of cultural diversity present in our society, and the similarities and differences in learning characteristics that can be found within any group of students. NAGC is fully committed to national goals that advocate both excellence and equity for all students, and we believe that the best way to achieve these goals is through differentiated educational opportunities, resources, and encouragement for all students.

The practice of grouping, enabling students with advanced abilities and/or performance to be grouped together to receive appropriately challenging instruction, has recently come under attack. NAGC wishes to reaffirm the importance of grouping for instruction of gifted students. Grouping allows for more appropriate, rapid, and advanced instruction, which matches the rapidly development skills and capabilities of gifted students.

Special attention should be given to the identification of gifted and talented students who may not be identified through traditional assessment methods (including economically disadvantaged individuals, individuals of limited English proficiency, and individuals with handicaps), to help them participate effectively in special grouping programs.

Strong research evidence supports the effectiveness of ability grouping for gifted students in accelerated classes, enrichment programs, advanced placement programs, etc. Ability and performance grouping has been used extensively in programs for musically and artistically gifted students, and for athletically talented students with little argument. Grouping is a necessary component of every graduate and professional preparation program, such as law, medicine, and the sciences. It is an accepted practice that is used extensively in the education programs in almost every country in the western world.

NAGC does not endorse a tracking system that sorts all children into fixed layers in the school system with little attention to particular content, student motivation, past accomplishment, or present potential.

To abandon the proven instructional strategy of grouping students for instruction at a time of educational crisis in the

U.S. will further damage our already poor competitive position with the rest of the world, and will renege on our promise to provide an appropriate education for all children.

Acceleration

Acceleration, or the rapid advancement of a student through the education system, has been used in various settings throughout most of the 20th century. After all, if youngsters have learned the material several grades in advance of their age placement, why shouldn't schools consider placing them with their intellectual peers rather than their age peers?

However, such a decision is not so simple. The physical and social development of the gifted child must also be taken into consideration, and such development is rarely as dramatically advanced as is the cognitive development. Still, for many gifted students, acceleration offers the opportunity for appropriately advanced curriculum and a head start onto the potentially long road of continuing education

Acceleration Position Statement

The National Association for Gifted Children (NAGC) periodically issues policy statements dealing with issues, policies, and practices that have an impact on the education of gifted and talented students. Policy statements represent the official convictions of the organization.

All policy statements approved by the NAGC Board of Directors are consistent with the organization's belief that education in a democracy must respect the uniqueness of all individuals, the broad range of cultural diversity present in our society, and the similarities and differences in learning characteristics that can be found within any group of students. NAGC is fully committed to national goals that advocate both excellence and equity for all students, and we believe that the best way to achieve these goals is through differentiated educational opportunities, resources, and encouragement for all students.

The practice of educational acceleration has long been used to match appropriate learning opportunities with student abilities. The goals of acceleration are to adjust the pace of instruction to the student's capability, to provide an appropriate level of challenge, and to reduce the time period necessary for students to complete traditional schooling. When acceleration has been effective in achieving these goals, highly capable individuals are prepared to begin contributing to society at an earlier age. Although instructional adaptations, such as compacting, telescoping, and curriculum revision, which allow more economic use of time are desirable practices for exceptionally talented students, there are situations in which such modifications are insufficient in fulfilling the academic potential of all highly capable children. Personal acceleration is called for in these cases.

Personal acceleration involves moving a student through the traditional educational organization more quickly and includes such practices as grade skipping, concurrent enrollment in two grades, early entrance into kindergarten or college, credit by examination, combining three years of middle school into two, acceleration in particular content areas, and dual enrollment in high school and college. Students may be accelerated in one discipline or across disciplines.

Research documents the academic benefits and positive outcomes of personal acceleration for carefully selected students. Decisions about the appropriateness of personal acceleration and the extent of acceleration for a given student should include examination of student preferences and disposition relative to the decision, the student's intellectual and academic profile, and social readiness. Other factors which enhance the success of personal acceleration are positive attitudes of teachers, timing of the decision, parent support, and the careful monitoring of new placements with a clearly articulated option to return to the earlier setting without penalty.

Opportunities to learn must be offered to all children. Accordingly, highly able students with capability and motivation to succeed in placements beyond traditional age/grade parameters should be provided the opportunity to enroll in intellectually appropriate classes and educational settings.

Addressing the Affective Needs of Gifted Children

The emotional needs of gifted students often seem to take second place to their academic progress. There is an additional assumption among some educators that if gifted students are doing well in the academic arenas, they should not have any special needs in emotional development.

This approach has resulted in the limited use of counseling and psychological support services for gifted students. Yet many of these students have problems with perfectionism, with intense feelings around moral and ethical issues, and deep concerns about social problems at an early age when they may not be emotionally equipped to cope with their own feelings. This position statement reminds educators of the wide range of emotional problems such students might have, and the need to see that students receive necessary help in this key area of development.

Addressing the Affective Needs of Gifted Children Position Paper

The National Association for Gifted Children (NAGC) periodically issues policy statements dealing with issues, policies, and practices that have an impact on the education of gifted and talented students. Policy statements represent the official convictions of the organization.

All policy statements approved by the NAGC Board of Directors are consistent with the organization's belief that education in a democracy must respect the uniqueness of all individuals, the broad range of cultural diversity present in our society, and the similarities and differences in learning characteristics that can be found within any group of students. NAGC is fully committed to national goals that advocate both excellence and equity for all students, and we believe that the best way to achieve these is through differentiated educational opportunities, resources, and encouragement for all students.

Educational and counseling programs must provide all children with opportunities to develop understanding of themselves and their role in society. Because, by definition, gifted children differ significantly from others, these programs should be responding to the social-emotional or affective characteristics that distinguish gifted students from others. Furthermore, since significant differences also exist within the gifted population, appropriate services need to be designed and implemented to respond to individual differences.

Characteristics such as emotional and moral intensity, sensitivity to expectations and feelings, perfectionism, lofty goals and standards for themselves and others, and deep concerns about societal problems at an early age are found in a proportionally higher incidence among gifted and talented children. Those who have disabilities or differ in other ways, including culturally, linguistically, or socioeconomically may have additional affective needs.

NAGC believes that gifted children also require appropriate affective services including gifted-focused counseling interventions and career-development guidance programs if they are to develop their potential. NAGC recommends that these services be designed to:

- Provide orientation to gifted programming, including information about the selection process and the social, emotional, and academic implications of the giftedness

- Enhance relationships with others, including both those who are identified as gifted and those who are not

- Assist with long-term life planning, including opportunities to deal with issues related to multi-potentiality

- Provide counseling that addresses the increased incidence of perfectionism, unrealistic goals, emotional intensity, moral concerns, and the resultant stress and lower achievement in the gifted population

Some gifted and talented children, because of heightened intellectual and social-emotional needs, may experience difficulties that require professional intervention. NAGC believes that it is imperative that those who provide services at such times have expertise in understanding the impact of giftedness on a child's development.

Competencies Needed by Teachers of Gifted and Talented Students

NAGC is concerned about the proper preparation and training of all teachers of gifted and talented students. The position paper provides some general guidance on the knowledge and skills necessary for these teachers to develop in order to meet the special educational needs and advanced development of gifted and talented students.

Competencies Needed by Teachers of Gifted and Talented Students Position Statement

The National Association for Gifted Children (NAGC) periodically issues policy statements dealing with issues, policies, and practices that have an impact on the education of gifted and talented students. Policy statements represent the official convictions of the organization.

All policy statements approved by the NAGC Board of Directors are consistent with the organization's belief that education in a democracy must respect the uniqueness of all individuals, the broad range of cultural diversity present in our society, and the similarities and differences in learning characteristics that can be found within any group of students. NAGC is fully committed to national goals that advocate both excellence and equity for all students, and we believe that the best way to achieve these goals is through differentiated educational opportunities, resources, and encouragement for all students.

NAGC believes that all children deserve the highest quality of instruction possible and that such instruction will only occur when teachers are aware of and able to respond to the unique qualities and characteristics of the students they instruct. Gifted and talented students present a particular challenge and often experience inadequate and inappropriate education. To provide appropriate learning experiences for gifted and talented students, teachers need to possess:

- a knowledge and valuing of the origins and nature of high levels of intelligence, including creative expressions of intelligence;
- a knowledge and understanding of the cognitive, social, and emotional characteristics, needs, and potential problems experienced by gifted and talented students from diverse populations;
- a knowledge of and access to advanced content and ideas;
- an ability to develop a differentiated curriculum appropriate to meeting the unique intellectual and emotional needs and interests of gifted and talented students; and
- an ability to create an environment in which gifted and talented students can feel challenged and safe to explore and express their uniqueness.

NAGC believes that these competencies, in addition to those required for good teaching and learning in general, such as modeling openness, curiosity, and enthusiasm, are necessary for teachers of gifted and talented students. NAGC also believes that educational experiences through comprehensive programming must be available for teachers to develop these competencies.

Cooperative Learning for Gifted Students

One of the most popular educational strategies of the 1990s is *cooperative learning*, a set of classroom practices that stresses small-group work around a common goal.

Some of the proponents of cooperative learning have emphasized the necessity of heterogeneous grouping in cooperative learning, requiring that gifted students always be placed in groups with average or below average students. This position statement, while applauding the general goals of cooperative learning, lays out some specific suggestions on how this strategy can best be used with gifted students.

Cooperative Learning for Gifted Students Position Paper

The National Association for Gifted Children (NAGC) periodically issues policy statements that deal with issues, policies, and practices that have an impact on the education of gifted and talented students. Policy statements represent the official conviction of the organization.

All policy statements approved by the NAGC Board of Directors are consistent with the organization's belief that education in a democracy must respect the uniqueness of all individuals, the broad range of cultural diversity present in our society, and the similarities and differences in learning characteristics that can be found within any group of students. NAGC is fully committed to national goals that advocate both excellence and equity for all students, and we believe that the best way to achieve these goals is through differentiated educational opportunities, resources, and encouragement for all students.

Cooperative Learning (CL) encompasses a variety of classroom practices which include the following attributes:

group interdependence built around common goals, a focus on social skills or group dynamics, and individual accountability for material learned. Cooperative learning experiences can provide valuable opportunities to share ideas, practice critical thinking, and gain social skills.

When heterogeneous CL groups are the primary strategy in the classroom, gifted students' needs may not be met. Cooperative learning advocates often stress forming CL groups with students intentionally clustered by mixed abilities. When gifted students are included in these CL groups, special care must be taken to differentiate the tasks appropriately. Cooperative learning is more likely to be effective for gifted learners when group tasks and goals:

- take into account differences in students' readiness levels, interests, and learning modes;
- focus on high level tasks that require students to manipulate, apply, and extend meaningful ideas;
- ensure appropriate and balanced work responsibilities for all participants;
- ensure balanced opportunities for learners to work with peers of similar as well as mixed readiness levels; and
- are balanced with opportunities for students to work independently and with the class as a whole.

When differentiation does not happen, gifted students may feel overburdened and responsible for the entire "workload."

Teachers who use CL with heterogeneous groups need additional support and preparation in how to structure the learning tasks to ensure that the instructional activities meet the cognitive and social needs of the most able students in the group.

NAGC believes that cooperative learning should be viewed within a range of instructional strategies that may enhance some learning objectives for some gifted students some of the time but should not be used as a panacea to replace differentiated services addressing the educational needs of gifted students. When used in conjunction with an array of services to differentiate the education of gifted students, CL can be an appropriate strategy.

Differentiation of Curriculum and Instruction

While educators of gifted students often say that the key to their instruction is "differentiation" from the regular curriculum, it is not often clear precisely what differentiation means in any given circumstance. Differentiated curriculum is necessary in order to meet the widely differing academic needs of individual students. In the case of gifted students, differentiation is essential in order to adjust course content for students' prior knowledge of the standard curriculum and to provide a challenging learning experience. This position statement explains what is meant by differentiated education, and what does not constitute differentiation when adjusting curriculum for gifted students.

Differentiation of Curriculum and Instruction Position Statement

The National Association for Gifted Children (NAGC) periodically issues policy statements dealing with issues, policies, and practices that have an impact on the education of gifted and talented students. Policy statements represent the official convictions of the organization.

All policy statements approved by the NAGC Board of Directors are consistent with the organization's belief that education in a democracy must respect the uniqueness of all individuals, the broad range of cultural diversity present in our society, and the similarities and differences in learning characteristics that can be found within any group of students. NAGC is fully committed to national goals that advocate both excellence and equity for all students, and we believe that the best way to achieve these goals is through differentiated educational opportunities, resources, and encouragement for all students.

NAGC supports the provision of appropriate quality educational experiences for all students across the spectrum of ability, background, and achievement. The learning needs of gifted students often differ from those of other students and should be addressed through differentiation, a modification of curriculum and instruction based on the assessed achievement and interests of individual students.

To provide appropriate and challenging educational experiences for gifted students, differentiation may include:

- acceleration of instruction;
- in-depth study;
- a high degree of complexity;
- advanced content; and/or
- variety in content and form

Problems occur when teachers attempt to meet the needs of gifted students by limiting learning experiences to:

- offering more of the same level of material or the same kind of problem;
- providing either enrichment or acceleration alone;

- focusing only on cognitive growth in isolation from affective, physical, or intuitive growth;
- teaching higher thinking skills (e.g. research or criticism) in isolation from academic content;
- presenting additional work that is just different from the core curriculum; and/or
- grouping with intellectual peers without differentiating content and instruction.

Differentiation for gifted students consists of carefully planned, coordinated learning experiences that extend beyond the core curriculum to meet the specific learning needs evidenced by the student. It combines the curricular strategies of enrichment and acceleration and provides flexibility and diversity. Appropriate differentiation allows for increasing levels of advanced, abstract, and complex curriculum that are substantive and that respond to the learner's needs. NAGC believes that the use of such differentiation is essential to maximize the educational experience for gifted and talented students. NAGC further believes that appropriate educational experiences for these students are more effective when differentiated materials and activities are planned in advance and easily accessible.

Fine Arts Education

In many schools, gifted education has been limited to programming that supports linguistic, science, and mathematical excellence. This position statement underscores the importance of the fine arts in a comprehensive program for gifted students. It makes the point that music, theatre, visual arts, and dance should not be considered an educational frill, but rather that the arts form an essential component in an excellent basic education.

Fine Arts Education Position Statement

The National Association for Gifted Children (NAGC) periodically issues policy statements that deal with issues, policies, and practices that have an impact on the education of gifted and talented students. Policy statements represent the official convictions of the organization.

All policy statements approved by the NAGC Board of Directors are consistent with the organization's belief that education in a democracy must respect the uniqueness of all individuals, the broad range of cultural diversity present in our society, and the similarities and differences in learning characteristics that can be found within any group of students. NAGC is fully committed to national goals that advocate both excellence and equity for all students, and we believe that the best way to achieve these goals is through differentiated educational opportunities, resources, and encouragement for all students.

Frequently, when school resources are limited, arts education funding is reduced or eliminated. Proponents of such cuts defend the action by referring to the arts as a valuable but nonessential element of an educational program designed primarily to develop basic skills. NAGC maintains that arts education is fundamental to an excellent basic education for all students and to an appropriately challenging curriculum for gifted students.

Arts education generally provides learning experiences through the art forms of music, visual art, theater, and dance. These experiences develop within students understandings of key arts principles of:

- history-with abilities to inquire into the contributions artists and art make to society and culture
- criticism-with abilities to make judgments about qualities and properties found in art forms

- aesthetics-with abilities to make personal and sound decisions about works of art, and
- production-with abilities to participate in the arts and to produce personal works of art with skill and creativity

The goal of arts education is to equip students with the knowledge and skills needed to understand and communicate clearly within their personal, community, and cultural environments. Schools with well-supported arts education also often report enhanced reading, writing, and math skills; improved critical and creative thinking; and increased commitment to learning, and heightened multicultural understanding.

Arts education can benefit artistically gifted students by introducing them to the multiple possibilities for expression with the arts, educating them in the skills of perception, production, and performance, and opening gateways to the various career paths in the arts. As well, arts education can benefit academically gifted students by increasing the complexity and rigor of the curriculum, promoting extensive use of a variety of problem-solving strategies, heightening student motivation to pursue a topic of interest in depth, and developing rich skills in communicating with varied audiences.

NAGC supports the principle that arts education is an essential component of a sound program leading to the achievement of fundamental educational goals. Further, NAGC encourages the identification of and provision of services for artistically gifted students, as well as the integration of fine arts education into programs for the gifted for the benefit of academically gifted students.

Inclusion

Inclusion is one of the current educational strategies implemented in many school districts across the country. Inclusion is based on a philosophical position that all children should be educated in the same setting. While this strategy was originated to meet the needs of children with disabilities, many school districts have begun to apply the same philosophy to programs and services for gifted and talented students.

This position statement lays out the special conditions that must be met for such a philosophy to address the needs of gifted students. Above all, it is essential to maintain the concept of differentiated education within inclusive classrooms in order to provide an appropriate education for all children.

Inclusion Position Statement

The National Association for Gifted Children (NAGC) periodically issues policy statements that deal with issues, policies, and practices that have an impact on the education of gifted and talented students. Policy statements represent the official conviction of the organization.

All policy statements approved by the NAGC Board of Directors are consistent with the organization's belief that education in a democracy must respect the uniqueness of all individuals, the broad range of cultural diversity present in our society, and the similarities and differences in learning characteristics that can be found within any group of students. NAGC is fully committed to national goals that advocate both excellence and equity for all students, and we believe that the best way to achieve these goals is through differentiated educational opportunities, resources, and encouragement for all students.

One of the many recent educational reforms affecting the field of special education has been that of *Inclusion*, which is the practice of educating children with disabilities in regular classrooms together with their non-disabled peers. This principle of *Inclusion* has recently been applied to gifted students in some educational settings.

NAGC maintains that gifted students, like other children with special needs, require a full continuum of educational services to aid in the development of the students' unique strengths and talents. One such option in that continuum of services for gifted students can be the regular classroom (inclusion). In such an inclusive setting there should be well-prepared teachers who understand and can program for these gifted students, and sufficient administrative support necessary to help differentiate the program to their special needs. There should be, for example, staff development to aid the general education teacher in understanding and instructing gifted students, provisions for teacher planning time, allowance for student independent study and access to a specialist in gifted education who can aid in differentiating the curriculum to meet the needs of advanced students.

NAGC supports the principle of excellence for all students and recognizes that there are many different models for educating students with special gifts; but all models, inclusion included, require a differentiated set of services that will allow these students to be challenged to be all they can be.

Mandated Educational Opportunities for Gifted and Talented Students

Over the years, states have mandated programs for gifted students but have left the determination of how to structure such programs to local school districts. The federal government has never mandated serving gifted and talented students.

As the focus on the special needs of gifted students has changed over the years, NAGC felt it important to call upon both the federal and the state governments to mandate programs and services that meet the needs of gifted students. This position statement calls on the nation to recognize and serve the special educational needs of gifted students that will allow them to reach their full potential.

Mandated Educational Opportunities for Gifted and Talented Students Position Statement

The National Association for Gifted Children (NAGC) periodically issues policy statements dealing with issues, policies, and practices that have an impact on the education of gifted and talented students. Policy statements represent the official convictions of the organization.

All policy statements approved by the NAGC Board of Directors are consistent with the organization's belief that education in a democracy must respect the uniqueness of all individuals, the broad range of cultural diversity present in our society, and the similarities and differences in learning characteristics that can be found within any group of students. NAGC is fully committed to national goals that advocate both excellence and equity for all students, and we believe that the best way to achieve these goals is through differentiated educational opportunities, resources, and encouragement for all students.

NAGC supports mandating services to meet the unique needs of gifted and talented children.

Numerous studies, including the federal report *National Excellence: A Case for Developing America's Talent*, released in November 1993, have documented that the needs of our nation's gifted and talented students are not being met. Programs for these students are currently often viewed as extracurricular and are available only on a limited basis in some school systems, money permitting. The needs of gifted and talented students have been well documented by research and federal studies.

To educate all our children and allow America to compete in a global economy and all fields of human endeavor, the nation must provide an environment in which gifted and talented students, along with all of our children, can reach their full potential.

Middle Schools

The movement toward developing age-appropriate middle level education has stressed the unique developmental challenges of students in grades 5 to 9. Key to much of the literature in that field has been attention to the affective needs of students, including positive and cooperative interactions with peers. NAGC, while supporting many of the principles underlying middle level education, also wishes to underscore the necessity of differentiation to meet individual needs within any general curriculum. This would include the need for various grouping patterns and instructional strategies to carry out differentiation at the middle level. It is hoped that commitment to the social and emotional life of the child does not result in a neglect of academic rigor and curriculum adaptations that are especially needed by gifted students at this age level.

Middle Schools Position Statement

The National Association for Gifted Children (NAGC) periodically issues policy statements dealing with issues, policies, and practices that have an impact on the education of gifted and talented students. Policy statements represent the official convictions of the organization.

All policy statements approved by the NAGC Board of Directors are consistent with the organization's belief that education in a democracy must respect the uniqueness of all individuals, the broad range of cultural diversity present in our society, and the similarities and differences in learning characteristics that can be found within any group of students. NAGC is fully committed to national goals that advocate both excellence and equity for all students, and we believe that the best way to achieve these goals is through *differentiated* educational opportunities, resources, and encouragement for all students.

NAGC applauds and supports the fundamental principles of the Middle School movement. We endorse in particular:

- an emphasis on individual student needs;
- teaching thinking strategies and decision-making;
- teacher as facilitator, rather than knowledge-giver;
- interdisciplinary curricula;
- encouraging students to work at their own pace;
- student membership in a "family" or home group;
- extension of learning beyond the textbooks.

In addition, NAGC believes that the flexible use of grouping for instruction and accelerated programs in content fields to match students' advanced abilities and knowledge can meet the needs of gifted students while maintaining the important social goals of the Middle School movement.

Preservice Teacher Education Programs

This statement complements the policy statement on competencies needed for teachers of gifted and talented students. Teachers who will spend a substantial amount of time with gifted and talented students in an academic setting, whether homogeneous or heterogeneous, need specific knowledge and skills in order to meet the goals of differentiated education. This policy statement outlines what NAGC believes teacher preparation programs should include to familiarize undergraduate education students to the characteristics and educational needs of gifted and talented students.

Preservice Teacher Education Programs Position Statement

The National Association for Gifted Children (NAGC) periodically issues policy statements that deal with issues, policies, and practices that have an impact on the education of gifted and talented students. Policy statements represent the official conviction of the organization.

All policy statements approved by the NAGC Board of Directors are consistent with the organization's belief that education in a democracy must respect the uniqueness of all individuals, the broad range of cultural diversity present in our society, and the similarities and differences in learning characteristics that can be found within any group of students. NAGC is fully committed to national goals that advocate both excellence and equity for all students, and we believe that the best way to achieve these goals is through differentiated educational opportunities, resources, and encouragement for all students.

In many classrooms, one-size-fits-all instruction is pervasive. At the same time, these classrooms are becoming more academically diverse and classroom teachers are being asked to be primary service providers for the full range of academic diversity-including students who are advanced well beyond their age peers. The role of preservice education programs in preparing educators to work effectively in academically diverse classrooms is critical to the success of public education, and to its capacity to maximize the potential of all learners.

NAGC supports the Interstate New Teacher Assessment and Support Consortium (INTASC) standards for preservice teachers that include: knowledge of subject matter and how to make it accessible to students; understanding how to foster learning and development; ability to create learning experiences adapted to the needs of diverse learners; use of teaching strategies that foster critical thinking, problem solving, and high levels of performance; ability to create a positive and purposeful learning environment; knowledge of how to promote effective communication and collaboration in the classroom; ability to plan instruction based on subject matter and student needs; curriculum goals and community context; understanding of and skill in using a wide variety of assessment strategies; ability to reflect on, evaluate and improve teaching and learning; and ability to collaborate with colleagues and parents to support student learning. Preservice education programs that adhere to these standards will model them in teacher education classes and employ them as benchmarks for novice teacher preparedness in preservice teaching practica.

Implicit in appropriate application of these standards to gifted learners are preservice programs that explicitly and continually address:

1. characteristics of high-ability learners, including those from culturally and economically diverse backgrounds and those who underachieve;

2. recognition of needs of high-ability learners in classroom settings;

3. understanding the interrelationship between appropriate instructional challenge, student motivation, and student achievement in high-ability students;

4. proactive development of meaningful learning experiences well beyond grade-level expectations;

5 continual assessment of student progress and adaptation of instructional options based on assessment data;

6. appropriate use of a variety of instructional strategies to provide advanced and extended learning opportunities;

7. management of multitask classrooms, and

8. approaches to reporting student progress that stress individual student growth rather than only comparison to a grade-level norm.

NAGC believes that all aspects of effective teacher preparation programs should stress the responsibility of teachers to address the varying cognitive and affective needs of academically diverse student populations and relentlessly promote the skills necessary to succeed in addressing that pivotal responsibility.

Using Tests To Identify Gifted Students

The history of the education of gifted students includes numerous instances in which the identification of these students has been based upon standardized intelligence test (IQ) results.

NAGC urges caution in using such a limited tool and suggests a more multifaceted identification approach. Particular attention should be paid to the relevance of the instruments used to the specific services to be provided, and to the cultural differences that many students bring to the educational setting.

Using Tests To Identify Gifted Students Position Statement

The National Association for Gifted Children (NAGC) periodically issues policy statements that deal with issues, policies, and practices that have an impact on the education of gifted and talented students. Policy statements represent the official conviction of the organization.

All policy statements approved by the NAGC Board of Directors are consistent with the organization's belief that education in a democracy must respect the uniqueness of all individuals, the broad range of cultural diversity present in our society, and the similarities and differences in learning characteristics that can be found within any group of students. NAGC is fully committed to national goals that advocate both excellence and equity for all students, and we believe that the best way to achieve these goals is through differentiated educational opportunities, resources, and encouragement for all students.

Most school districts use some form of standardized achievement, intelligence, or creativity tests in the identification and screening process for gifted programs and services. When used properly and when selected with care, these instruments may provide valuable information about students' abilities, including their strengths and weaknesses. Tests are also valuable for assessing students' needs, and for designing programs and services based on these needs. Despite their potential usefulness, tests also have limitations. Testing instruments are not perfect or infallible predictors of intelligence, achievement, or ability and should be selected and used carefully. While critically important in all assessment, this precaution must be given even greater consideration when assessing underserved gifted students (i.e., young children, culturally diverse students, linguistically diverse students, economically disadvantaged students, and students with other special educational needs).

Given the limitations of all tests, no single measure should be used to make identification and placement decisions. That is, no single test or instrument should be used to include a child in or exclude a child from gifted education services. The most effective and equitable means of serving gifted students is to assess them to identify their strengths and weaknesses, and to prescribe services based on these needs. Testing situations should not hinder students' performance. Students must feel comfortable, relaxed, and have a good rapport with the examiner. Best practices indicate that multiple measures and valid indicators from multiple sources must be used to assess and serve gifted students. Information should be gathered from multiple sources (caregivers/families, teachers, students, and others with significant knowledge of the students), in different ways (e.g., observations, performances, products, portfolios, interviews), and in different contexts (e.g., in-school and out-of-school settings).

Any school personnel who administer, use, or advise others in the use of standardized tests should be qualified to do so. They should:

1. Understand measurement principles, including how to evaluate the test's technical claims (e.g., validity and reliability);
2. Know about the particular test used, its appropriate uses, and its limitations, including possible consequences resulting from scores;

3. Administer, score, and interpret results in a professional and responsible manner;
4. Employ procedures necessary to reduce or eliminate bias in test selection, administration, and interpretation;
5. Understand the influence of cultural diversity, linguistic diversity, and socioeconomic disadvantages on test performance; and
6. Weigh the results of tests carefully with other information.

NAGC advocates that all school personnel continue to explore, adapt, and evaluate comprehensive assessment alternatives to ensure that all gifted students are given an equal opportunity to develop their potential.

Standards for Graduate Programs in Gifted Education

Graduate programs in gifted and talented education should develop knowledge, skills, and dispositions beyond those demanded by general education classroom teachers who teach gifted students in a heterogeneous setting.

The standards presented here represent model elements for graduate programs in gifted education where the goal is to provide additional specific expertise for teachers who already have obtained general elementary or secondary certification. These standards address the necessary conceptual framework, characteristics of graduate students, and the range of professional education faculty that would be required for an exemplary graduate program.

Standard for Graduate Programs in Gifted Education Position Statement

The National Association for Gifted Children (NAGC) periodically issues policy statements dealing with issues, policies, and practices that have an impact on the education of gifted and talented students. Policy statements represent the official convictions of the organization.

All policy statements approved by the NAGC Board of Directors are consistent with the organization's belief that education in a democracy must respect the uniqueness of all individuals, the broad range of cultural diversity present in our society, and the similarities and differences in learning characteristics that can be found within any group of students. NAGC is fully committed to national goals that advocate both excellence and equity for all students, and we believe that the best way to achieve these goals is through differentiated educational opportunities, resources, and encouragement for all students.

Standards for Graduate Programs in Gifted Education, attached, include:

1. Conceptual Framework;
2. Candidates for Graduate Programs in Gifted Education;
3. Professional Education Faculty; and
4. Resources

Standard for Graduate Programs in Gifted Education

Category I: Conceptual Framework

(A) Conceptual Framework

The graduate program in gifted education is based on a conceptual framework derived from research on the nature of giftedness, the unique needs of gifted and talented persons, and the methodologies best suited to meeting these needs.

Indicators:

(1) The conceptual framework of the program includes a clear articulation of the philosophy, goals, and knowledge base of the curriculum.

(2) The courses and field experiences that comprise the curriculum are consistent with the conceptual framework.

(B) Professional Studies

The program provides graduate program candidates with professional coursework and field experiences designed to develop specialists who are proficient within the field of gifted education.

Indicators:

The curriculum incorporates into the required course work and field experiences an integrated series of activities designed to develop in its graduates the following concepts and skills:

(1) Knowledge and understanding of

(a) principles of human development and the nature of individual differences, especially as applied to exceptional abilities

(b) the origins and nature of various types and manifestations of giftedness

(c) the cognitive, social, emotional, and environmental factors that enhance or inhibit the development of giftedness in all populations

(d) a variety of methods for identifying and assessing students with extraordinary potential

(e) the historical and theoretical foundations of the field of gifted education, current trends and issues, and potential future directions of the field

(f) current and seminal research related to learning theory, giftedness, and creativity

(g) a research-based rationale for differentiated programming for gifted students

(h) theoretical models, program prototypes, and educational principles that offer appropriate foundations for the development of differentiated curriculum for gifted students

(i) the unique potentials of gifted students from underserved populations, including but not limited to gifted females and those who are disabled, racially or ethnically diverse, economically disadvantaged, and/or underachieving

(j) advanced concepts in a variety of areas, including in-depth studies in content and processes that are appropriate to the anticipated professional roles of individual candidates

(k) current educational issues, policies and practices and their relationships to the field of gifted education

(l) the influence of the social, cultural, political and economic environment on the field of gifted education

(m) the interdependent relationships between general education and gifted education

(2) The ability to

(a) interpret and apply knowledge related to the nature and needs of gifted students

(b) identify and assess the unique needs of gifted students

(c) design, implement, facilitate, and evaluate differentiated learning experiences for gifted students

(d) create an environment in which giftedness can emerge and gifted students can feel challenged and safe to explore and express their uniqueness

(e) develop differentiated curricula to meet the unique intellectual, academic, and social-emotional needs of gifted students

(f) use effectively such techniques as grouping for appropriate instruction and individualized planning to assist gifted students in realizing their unique potentials

(g) integrate instruction in a variety of fields to encourage interdisciplinary thought and studies of gifted students

(h) use emerging technologies in research and in the teaching of gifted students

(i) modify curriculum to allow time for gifted students to pursue their interests with depth and breadth

(j) vary teaching styles and instructional strategies to help gifted students meet their individual needs

(k) develop in gifted students the attitudes and skills needed to become independent, life-long leaders, to self-evaluate, and to set and pursue appropriate personal and academic goals for future success

(l) utilize current, research-based methods for assessing and reporting on the progress of gifted students for the purpose of making differentiated educational decisions

(m) provide consultation, collaboration, and staff development services in gifted education for teachers and administrators in the general education program

(n) communicate and work in partnerships with colleagues, administrators, students, families, business and industry, and the public, in advocating appropriate programming for gifted students

(o) act as a change agent in the social, cultural, political, and economic environments inhibiting services to gifted students

(p) foster partnerships with the families of gifted students in order to facilitate a total learning environment

(q) forge an integrated program of excellence between general education and gifted education

(C) Field Experiences

The field experiences required in the graduate program are consistent with the conceptual framework, are well planned and sequenced, and are of high quality.

(1) Field experiences, practica, and internships in the gifted education program are sufficiently extensive and intensive to prepare individual candidates for effective performance in the roles for which they are preparing.

(2) Field experiences are provided in a variety of settings that expose students to the diversity that exists within the gifted population.

(3) Field experiences are designed to provide candidates with opportunities to

(a) observe master teachers providing direct and indirect services to gifted students;

(b) relate principles and theories from the conceptual framework to actual practice in the field of gifted education;

(c) study, observe, plan instruction for, and provide direct services to gifted students of different ages and cultural backgrounds.

Standards for Graduate Programs in Gifted Education (continued)

Category II: Candidates for Graduate Programs in Gifted Education

(A) Entrance Qualifications and Composition

The institution recruits, admits and retains candidates who demonstrate potential for professional success in the field of gifted education and encourages application and matriculation of students from diverse backgrounds.

Indicators:

(1) Recruitment efforts and admission standards are designed to attract a high quality of students.

(2) Recruitment efforts and admission standards are designed to attract students from diverse backgrounds.

(3) Criteria for admission to graduate programs in gifted education consider a variety of indicators such as appropriate test data, records of academic achievement, evidence of suc-

cessful teaching experience, and other current methods of assessing academic and teaching potential.

(B) Assessment and Exit Criteria

The faculty systematically monitors and assesses the progress of candidates to ensure that they receive appropriate academic and professional advisement from admission through completion of their graduate program in gifted education.

Indicators:

(1) Criteria used in the assessment of student progress are consistent with the philosophy and goals articulated in the conceptual framework of the program.

(2) The program employs defensible means for monitoring, reporting, and facilitating student progress that are appropriate to the goals of the program and are consistent with current practice in assessment.

(3) The program provides follow-up evaluation and services for its graduates.

Standards for Graduate Programs in Gifted Education (continued)

Category III: Professional Education Faculty

(A) Qualifications and Composition

The professional education faculty who teach graduate courses in gifted education represent or are knowledgeable about diverse cultures and are well qualified to provide instruction and design course work and field experiences for persons preparing for careers in the field.

Indicators:

(1) Efforts are made to recruit gifted education faculty from diverse backgrounds.

(2) Graduate programs in gifted education employ faculty with professional and scholarly identification in the field.

(3) The quality of the faculty is commensurate with other high quality programs in the institution and within the field of gifted education.

(4) Each faculty member who serves as a graduate advisor or chairs thesis/dissertation committees possesses an earned doctorate, has demonstrated competence in educational research, and is knowledgeable about current theories and practices related to the field.

(5) Gifted program practitioners who supervise field experiences hold appropriate credentials to evaluate the performance of candidates, have had appropriate professional training and teaching experiences, and have demonstrated competence to serve in this capacity. Such persons model instructional and affective practices that are congruent with the philosophy and goals of the program.

(B) Scholarly Activity

Faculty with primary responsibilities for graduate training in gifted education maintain a high level of scholarly activity.

Indicators:

Gifted education faculty

(1) Maintain a high level of scholarship through such activities as research, publication, and presentation at professional meetings;

(2) Are actively involved in professional associations within and beyond the field of gifted education;

(3) Collaborate with colleagues and practitioners in research, teaching, and placement and assessment of candidates for graduate programs in gifted education.

Standards for Graduate Programs in Gifted Education *(continued)*

Category IV: Resources

Professional assignments and resources allow active faculty involvement in teaching, scholarship, and service.

Indicators:

(1) Faculty assignments allow time for high quality teaching, scholarship, and service.

(2) Faculty teaching loads are consistent with the requirements of the National Council for the Accreditation of Teacher Education.

(3) Human, financial, technological, library, and other media resources are sufficient to support quality instruction and scholarly activity.

About the Authors

Dr. Frances A. Karnes is Professor of Special Education and Director of the Center for Gifted Studies at The University of Southern Mississippi where she has been a member of the faculty since being awarded the Ph.D. degree by the University of Illinois in 1973. She has become widely known for her research, publications, innovative program developments and service activities in gifted education and leadership training. Dr. Karnes is author or co-author of more than 185 papers published in scholarly journals, numerous monographs and book chapters, and is co-author of fifteen books in gifted education and related areas.

Legal issues that arise as parents, educators and other advocates seek appropriate educational opportunities for gifted and talented children are addressed by Dr. Karnes and her colleague and co-author, Dr. Ronald G. Marquardt, in twenty of their journal articles. Legal problems and alternate approaches to their resolution are explored in depth in two of their previous books that enjoy wide circulation and are frequently cited: *Gifted Children and the Law: Mediation, Due Process and Court Cases* and *Gifted Children and Legal Issues in Education: Parents' Stories of Hope.*

Dr. Karnes is extensively involved in the affairs of the university she represents and also maintains an active role in civic and professional organizations in her community, state and nation. She presents papers annually at state and national conferences conducted by professional associations, and provides service to institutions and agencies throughout the country as a consultant. For many years she has been an active member of the editorial boards of several professional journals. She has served as president in two state professional organizations and as president and in several other elective positions of The Association of the Gifted of the Council for Exceptional Children. Currently, she is vice-president of the Hattiesburg Area Education Foundation, serves on the Board of Directors of the National Association for Gifted Children, the National Operational Volunteer Board of the Girl Scouts of the United States of America, and as member of the Board of Trustees of Quincy University at Quincy, Illinois.

Honors received by Dr. Karnes include: Faculty Research Award extended by The University of Southern Mississippi Alumni Association, Honorary Doctor of Education Degree bestowed by Quincy University, The University of Southern Mississippi Professional Service Award, and The University of Southern Mississippi Basic Research Award, and an award presented by the Mississippi Legislature for outstanding contributions to academic excellence in higher education. Additionally, she was presented the Distinguished Alumni Award from the College of Education of the University of Illinois at Urbana-Champaign.

Dr. Ronald G. Marquardt is currently Professor and Chair of the Department of Political Science at The University of Southern Mississippi. He possesses B.S. and M.S. degrees from Kansas State College, and received his Ph.D. from the University of Missouri. He was awarded his J.D. degree from Mississippi College School of Law where he graduated "with distinction" and where he has taught as a visiting professor. Dr. Marquardt, a specialist in constitutional and administrative law, has published numerous articles in such diverse journals as the Law and Policy

Quarterly, Midwest Quarterly, Mississippi Folklore Register, The College Student Affairs Journal, Law Library Journal, Journal of Paralegal Education, Administrative Law Review, Roeper Review, and the Peabody Journal of Education. In addition to his duties as Political Science Chair, he has also served as Director of Paralegal Studies, Faculty Athletics Representative, Pre-law Advisor for the College of Liberal Arts, and Legal Services Attorney for the Associated Study Body Legal Services Office.

Index

A

Ability Grouping Position Statement   173
Abuse   21, 55, 92, 99, 102-103
Accelerated   30, 38, 74, 98, 174, 176, 193
Acceleration Position Statement   175
Accident Cases   83-84, 88
Accreditation of Teacher Education   208
ACLU   125
Administrative
   Code Committee   25-26
   Law Review   211
   Procedures Act   27
Admissions   21-22, 28, 34, 110
Advanced Placement   101, 125, 174
Advocacy Association   162
Affective Needs of Gifted Children Position Paper   178
African Americans   112

AGATE   161-162
Age Discrimination Act   109
Alabama
   Association   157
   Special Education Services   143
Alaska Gifted   71, 143
American
   Association   167
   Civil Liberties Union   125
   Samoa   120
   University   85-86
AOL   158-159
Appeal   20, 35, 37, 39, 47, 50, 52, 100
Appealable   46
Appealed   24, 35, 37, 39-40, 52, 86, 99, 102
Application   33, 54, 131-132, 195, 205
Applications   90, 132, 136-137
Appropriate Placement   72-75, 79
Aptitude   2

Arizona
  Association 157
  Court of Appeals 50
  Department of Education 144
  Industrial Commission 50, 58, 140
  Workers Compensation Law 51
Arkansas
  Court of Appeals 95
  Office of Gifted 144
Articles 49, 209-210
Artistic 3, 90
Artistically 174, 188
Artists 187
Associated Study Body Legal Services Office 211
Athletic 99-100, 122
Athletically 174
Athletics 110, 122, 211
Atlanta Office U. S. Department of Education 118

Board of
  Directors 8, 171-173, 175, 178, 180, 182, 185, 187, 189, 191, 193-194, 197, 200, 210
  Education 14, 17, 22, 25-28, 32-33, 43-44, 55, 58-59, 67, 71, 80, 123, 139-141, 146-147
  Public Education 25-26, 28, 43-44, 140-141
  Trustees of Quincy University 210
Boston Office U. S. Department of Education 117
Brandin 102-103
Broadley 14, 17, 22-24, 43, 139
Brooke 87-89, 94
Brown 46-47, 106
Brownsville Area School District 36, 43, 139
Brunelle 124, 128, 139
Busing 45

B

Bellevue 164
Bennett 14, 17, 24-25, 43, 139
Bias Suit 125, 127

C

Caldwell School 41
California
  Association 158
  gifted 144, 158
Campo 84, 89, 107, 141
Career-development 179
Carpenter 100, 107, 139

Index

Cassel 55, 58, 140
Categories 24, 29, 77, 90-91
Catholic 46
Caucasian 112
Centennial School District V. Commonwealth Department Education 58
Certification 6-7, 11, 45, 48, 53-55, 57, 121, 199
Certified 113
Certify 78
Chancellor 95
Checklists 66
Chester-Upland School District 45-46, 58, 140
Chicago Office U. S. Department of Education 119
Child
 custody 84, 90, 92-94, 97-104
 support 83, 90-92, 94-95, 99, 104
Christian School 92-93
Civil Rights
 Act 32-33, 109
 Customer Service Team 116
Cleveland Office U. S. Department of Education 119
Cold Springs Center 32
College Expenses 47, 94-96
College of Education 91, 94, 104, 168, 210
College Liberal Arts 211

Colorado
 Association 158
 gifted 144, 158
Commissioner of Education 2
Commonwealth
 Board of Education 22, 43, 139
 court 35, 37, 39-40, 46-47, 54
compensation 49-51, 72, 77
competencies needed 180, 194
Conceptual Framework 199-201, 204-206
Congress 3, 11, 129, 137, 154
Connecticut
 Association 158
 gifted 23, 65, 145
 Supreme Court 24
Conrad Weiser School District 40, 43, 139
Consortium of Ohio Coordinators 162
Cooperative Learning 133, 182-184
Coral Way Elementary School 84
Cortines 16-17, 140
Court of Appeals 16, 20, 24, 50, 52, 55, 84, 86, 91, 95-97, 99, 101-103, 122
Crofton 160
Current Status of Mediation 65

215

Curriculum
Modification 34, 42, 121, 185
Services
Georgia Department of Education 146
Massachusetts Department of Education 148

D

Dallap 53-54, 58, 139
Dallas Office U. S. Department of Education 118
Dance 92, 186-187
Deaf 41
Delaware
gifted 145, 158
talented 145, 158
Denver Office U. S. Department of Education 120
Department of Political Science 210
Departments of Education 5, 65-67
Desegregation 28, 30
Dickison 101, 107, 139
Differentiation of Curriculum 184-185
Dilley 54, 58, 139
Disabilities
Act 16, 37, 39, 63, 109
Education Act 37, 39, 63

Disability 38, 40, 109, 111, 113-114
Disadvantaged 130, 136, 174, 198, 202
Discrimination Complaint Form 111
Distinguished Alumni Award 210
District of Columbia
Court of Appeals 86
gifted 145
Office U. S. Department of Education 118
Divorces 94
Domestic Relations Cases 90, 104
Due Process 9, 13-14, 20-21, 35, 37-38, 41, 46, 57, 59, 61, 65-66, 69, 71-75, 77, 79-81, 106, 112, 121-122, 209
Duran 124, 128, 140
Durham 167
Dyslexic 15

E

East Indians 112
Eastern District of New York 15
Easton Area School District 34-35, 43, 140

Ector County
  Board of Trustees 20
  Independent School District
    20, 44, 141
Educating 123, 133, 188, 190
Education
  amendments 1, 109
  Assistance Act 132, 135
  Law Reporter 57
  of gifted 6-7, 11, 14, 16, 19,
    22-23, 25-26, 34-36, 40,
    48, 55, 59, 115, 131-134,
    137, 143-145, 147-157,
    172-173, 175, 178, 180,
    182, 184, 187, 189, 191,
    193-194, 196-197, 200-
    202, 205, 207
Educational Amendments 11
EEOC 51-52
EFSS 168
Egan 55, 58, 140
Eighth Circuit Court of Appeals
  52
Eleventh Amendment 33
Ellis 45-47, 56, 58, 140
Enforcement Offices 110, 116
English 53, 75, 112, 174
Enhanced Educational
  Opportunities 100
Enrichment 35, 37-38, 75-76,
  174, 185-186
Enrollment 29, 31, 54, 91, 99,
  122, 176
Entrance Qualifications 205

Equal
  Employment Opportunity
    Commission 51
  Protection Clause 14, 30,
    32, 125
ERIC Clearinghouse 167
Establishment of National
  Center 134
Europe 91
Exceptional
  children 10-11, 23-24, 167,
    210
  Education Florida Education
    Center 145
Exit Criteria 206

F

Faculty
  athletics representative 211
  Research Award 210
Families 130, 149, 198, 204
Federal
  definitions 1
  Government 1, 16, 130, 190
Financing 9, 56, 123
Fine Arts Education Position
  Statement 187
First Amendment 15, 92, 123,
  125
Florida
  Association 158
  Bureau of Student Services
    145
  Court of Appeals 84

Fourteenth Amendment 14, 30, 125
Fourth Amendment 124
Fowler 40-43, 140
Freedom of Information Act 112
Funding 5, 91, 187
Funds 1, 5, 96, 110, 123, 131-134

G

GAGC 158
GED 79
Gender 14, 28, 113, 133
Gender-neutral 97
Geneva College 47
Georgia
  Association 158
  gifted education 146
Gifted
  Amherst County Public Schools 164
  Association of Missouri 161
  Child
    Society 167
    Today 69
  Children Lawrence County Education Service Center Courthouse 162
  Education
    Position Statement 200
    specialist 31, 190
    The Council 11, 167
  ESU 161
  Hamilton County Educational Service Center 162
  Psychology Press 57, 69, 81, 106
  Students
    Institute Southern Methodist University 168
    Position Paper 180, 182
    Studies 203, 209
  Teachers 7, 11, 31, 48-54, 57, 63, 163, 180-181, 194, 199, 204
  Virginia Department of Education 155
Global 8, 192
Goldman 103, 107, 140
Goza 99, 107, 140
Grade-level 196
Grades 31-32, 35, 55, 175-176, 192
Graduate Programs 199-201, 205-208
Grouping 29, 75, 77, 173-174, 182, 186, 192-193, 203
Guardian 87, 101
Guidance 47, 52, 110, 179-180
Guideline 9
Guthrie
  Board of Education 123
  Independent School District 141
  School District 128, 141
Guyer 66, 69

H

Harvard 48
Hawaii
  Gifted Association 158
  Student Support Services
    Hawaii Department of
    Education 146
Hechler 27, 44, 141
Henmon-Nelson Test of Mental
  Abilities 32
Heterogeneous 182-183, 194,
  199
Hicks 66, 69
High Potential 62
High-ability 150, 195-196
Highly Gifted 23, 30, 32, 38,
  95, 98
Hispanic 30
Historically 1, 97
Hoefers 92, 107, 140
Hollis 161
Homeschooling 15, 79, 121-
  124
Homogeneous 75, 194
Howard 92, 107, 140
Howell 85, 89, 107, 139

I

Idaho Special Education
  Services 146
IDEA 10, 16, 23-24, 89, 92
Illinois
  Association 159
  gifted 146, 159
Impaired 41-42
Improvement
  Department of Public
    Instruction 152
  of elementary 129
Inclusion Position Statement
  189
Indian Self-Determination
  132, 135
Indiana
  Association 159
  gifted 6, 97, 147
Individualized
  Education Plan 38-39, 41,
    46
  educational 9, 23, 73
Industrial
  Commission of Arizona 50,
    58, 140
  Park Road Middletown 145
Instruction Position Statement
  184
Instructional 48, 59, 74, 131,
  148, 174, 176, 183-184,
  192, 196, 203, 207
INTASC 195
Integrated 78, 201, 204

Intellectual 2-3, 6, 40-41, 87, 90-92, 104, 125-126, 175-176, 179, 181, 186, 203
Intellectually 35, 88-91, 98, 104, 124, 177
Intelligence 74, 76, 88, 181, 196-198
Intensity 178-179
Interdependence 183
Interdependent 202
Interdisciplinary 193, 203
Internet 16
Iowa gifted 147, 159
IQ 196
Issuance 22, 25, 27, 33, 89

J

Jackson 149, 161
Jacob Javits Gifted 3, 11, 129, 131, 133, 135, 137
Jefferson 36-37, 144, 149
Johnson 55, 58, 140
Jones 92, 107, 140
Journal of Paralegal Education 211
Judge
   Byer 36
   Wright 29-30
Judges 14, 23, 56, 91, 98, 100, 104
Judicial 13, 25-26, 56, 98, 104

Judiciaries 13
Jurisdiction 35, 72, 86
Jurisprudence 25, 98
Jury 85

K

Kahle 98, 108, 141
Kan 43, 107, 139-140
Kanouff 37
Kansas
   Association 159
Karouff 44, 141
Kay 66, 69
Kent State University College of Education 168
Kentucky
   Association 160
   Gifted 147, 160
Key 9, 40, 60-61, 92, 126, 177, 184, 187, 192
Keyes 28, 30, 43, 140
Kindergarten 19-21, 38, 55, 176
King 92-93
Krementz 85, 106

L

Law Library Journal 211
Legal
 Issues Related 83, 85, 87, 89, 91, 93, 95, 97, 99, 101, 103, 105, 107, 209
 Process 13, 15, 17, 121
 Services Attorney 211
Legislation 0-1, 4, 9, 157
Legislature 20, 25-26, 56, 210
LEXIS 107-108, 128, 139-141
Liability 87-88, 90, 93, 96
Library 73, 124, 208, 211
Limitations 52, 56, 197-198
Limited English 130, 136
Lincoln 49, 98, 150, 152
Lindbergh School District 51, 58, 141
Linguistic 186, 199
Linguistically 179, 198
Litigation 16, 30, 36, 38, 48, 56, 66, 94, 100
Little 106, 144, 174
Logue 103, 107, 140
Lombardo 103, 107, 140
Lorentzen 50-51, 58, 140
Louisiana Gifted 148
Lynn Public School 128, 139

M

Maine
 Educators 160
 gifted 148
Malloy 94, 107, 140
Mandamus 20, 22
Mandate 5, 7, 24-26, 191
Mandated Educational
 Opportunities 7, 190-191
Marland 2, 6, 11
Marriage 94, 96, 99, 102
Mary Baldwin College 94
Maryland
 Coalition 160
 Student Achievement 148
Massachusetts
 Association 160
 instructional 148
Mathematics 73, 75, 88, 173
McEntire 94, 107, 140
Mediation
 Process 57, 61, 63-67, 69, 79, 81, 106, 121, 209
 Resources 65
Medical 85-86, 126
Membership 157, 193
Mentor 98
Mentoring 133, 136
Meriden School District 23
Methodologies 201
Michigan
 Alliance 160
 Court of Appeals 103

Curriculum Development
   Program 149
Middle Schools Position
   Statement 192
Minnesota
   Council 160
   Office of Teaching 149
Minorities 31, 113
Minority 31, 33
Mississippi
   Association 161, 210
   College School of Law 210
   gifted 149, 161
   Legislature 210
Missouri Gifted Education
   Programs 149
Mitchell 163
Montana
   Administrative Code
   Commission 25, 43
   Committee 26
   Association 161
   Attorney General 27
   Board of Public Education
     25, 43, 140
   Constitution 26-27
   First Judicial District Court
     26
   Gifted Education Services
     150
Montgomery
   Board of Education 32-33
County
   Board of Education 32-33
   Public Schools 28, 32-33, 43
Moore 87-88, 107, 141
Morgan 101
Motivation 174, 177, 188, 196
Multicultural 188
Multidisciplinary 35, 46, 77
Murch Summer Discovery
   Program 85, 87, 93
Music 90, 186-187

N

Nachtman 54
NAGC Divisions 171
National
   Associations 15, 167, 169
   Center 1, 134, 168
   Council 208
   excellence 8, 11, 191
   Position Statements 171-208
   Research Center 1, 134, 168
   Talent Network 168
Native
   Americans 112
   Hawaiian 132
Nebraska
   Association 161
   Court of Appeals 99
   Supreme Court 49

Index

Negligence 86, 88-89
Neil Broadley 23-24
Network News Quarterly 163
Nevada
   Association 161
   gifted 150, 161
New Brighton Area School
   District 45, 47, 58, 141
New Hampshire
   Association 161
   Office of Gifted Education 150
New Jersey
   Association 161
   Gifted 151, 161
New Mexico Special Education Department 151
New Rochelle School District 17, 24, 43, 139
New York
   Office U. S. Department of Education 117
   State Phoenicia Elementary School 162
   Supreme Court 95, 122
Noncompliance 78
Nondiscriminatory 9, 28, 113, 121
Nonprofit 130, 133, 136-137
Normandale 160
North Carolina
   Association 162
North Dakota
   Curriculum Leadership 152
   Supreme Court 91
Northwest Gifted Child Association 164

O

Office for Civil Rights 115-116, 118
   Atlanta 118
   Boston 117
   Chicago 119
   Cleveland 119
   Dallas 118
   Denver 120
   Kansas City 119
   NewYork 117
   Philadelphia 117
   SanFrancisco 120
   Seattle 120
Office of Educational Research 11, 135, 137
Office of Gifted 1, 144, 150
Ohio Division of Special Education Ohio Department of Education 152
Oklahoma
   Association 162
   gifted 152, 162
Oregon
   Association 163
   Department of Education 66, 152
   gifted 152
Overview of State Legislation 4

P

Payment 47, 56, 91-93
Peabody Journal of Education 211
Pennsylvania
 Association 163
 Commonwealth Court 35, 37, 40, 47, 54
 Gifted Technical Assistance Program Bureau of Special Education 153
 Supreme Court 48, 53
Petition 35, 98, 101
Phi Delta Kappan 11
Placement 38, 47, 59, 72-77, 79, 101, 103, 125, 174-175, 198, 207
Policy Quarterly 210-211
Position
 Paper 7, 178, 180, 182
 Statement 173, 175, 177, 180, 182, 184, 186-187, 189, 191-192, 194, 197, 200
 statements 171, 173, 175, 177, 179, 181, 183, 185, 187, 189, 191, 193, 195, 197, 199, 201, 203, 205, 207
Precedent 23, 27, 33, 38-39, 52, 54
Preservation Teacher Education Programs Position Statement 194
Preserve Teacher Education Programs 194
Principal 46, 53, 60, 85, 87, 89
Private Schools 47, 56, 92, 130, 133
Proactive 66, 196
Proceeding 15, 98, 102-103
Proceedings 35, 71, 92
Professional Studies 201
Professor of Special Education 209
Program Eligibility 72, 76
Programs of National Significance 129
Psychological 74, 77, 177
Psychologist 46, 59, 77-78
Public Education 7, 25-26, 28, 43-44, 48, 76-77, 123, 131-132, 136, 140-141, 171, 195
Punxsutawney Area School District 36-37, 44, 141

Q

Quincy University 210

R

Race 14, 28-29, 109, 111, 113-114, 125
Racebased 34
Racially 202

Rather 14, 20, 28, 113, 175, 186, 193, 196
Recommendation 36, 50, 97
Recommendations 66, 80
Recruitment 110, 205
References 11, 24, 43, 57, 62, 69, 81, 106, 115, 127, 135
Rehabilitation Act 109
Reimbursement 47, 74-77
Religion 28, 93, 123, 125
Relocation 99, 101
Remedies 15-16, 39, 46, 52-53
Remedy 25, 36-39, 42, 49, 51
Renzulli 6, 11
Research 1, 8, 11, 16, 83, 124, 130-131, 134-135, 137, 168, 174, 176, 186, 192, 201-203, 207, 209-210
Resident 21, 29, 96, 102
Residential 83, 92, 95, 101
Resources 8, 42, 47-48, 65, 100, 110, 126, 130, 167, 169, 172, 174, 176, 178, 180, 182, 185, 187, 189, 191, 193-194, 197, 200, 208
Responsibilities 5, 9, 59, 110, 183, 207
Responsibility 93, 110, 196
Reynolds 49, 56, 58, 141
Rhode Island
 gifted 153
 State Advisory Committee 163
Richard 24, 98-99
Richbourg 102, 108, 141
Roeper Review 11, 57, 81, 115, 211
Rohn 96, 107, 141
Roscoe 101-102
Rosenfeld 28, 31, 33-34, 43, 141
Roswell 158
Ruling 27, 35, 74, 78-79, 91, 95, 102
Rulings 77, 126

S

Sahagun 127
Scholarly Activity 207-208
Scholarship 46, 207-208
School
 Board of Dade County 84, 107, 141
 District
  Hearings Subsection 66
 of Omaha 49, 58, 141
 Policies 45, 47, 49, 51, 53, 55, 57
 Policies Affecting Gifted Education 45
Schooling 36-37, 74, 77, 92-93, 176

Science 47, 73, 88, 186, 210-211
Scott 92, 108, 141
Seattle Office U. S. Department of Education 120
Secondary Schools 24, 129, 131, 136
Segregation 29-31
SENG 168
Seniority 48, 53-54
Sex 109, 111, 114
Shapiro 95, 108, 141
Sharon City School District 53, 58, 139
Shawnee Mission Association 102
Simmons 28-31, 44, 141
Slippery Rock Area School District 54, 58, 139
Sobol 121, 128, 139
Social-emotional 178-179, 203
Socialization 133
Societal 30, 178
Socioeconomic 30-31, 125, 199
South Carolina
 Consortium 163
 Office of Technology Assistance 153

South Dakota
 Association 163
 Gifted Education South Dakota Department of Education 153
 Miami Elementary School 84
Special Appeals
 Panel 35, 37, 39-40, 46-47
 Review Panel 46-47
 Due Process Appeals Review Panel 46
 needs 4, 77, 90-91, 126, 130-131, 177, 180, 190-191, 198
 Panel 35, 37, 39-40, 47
Specialist 31, 54, 190, 210
Specialists 9, 201
Stable Education Environment 101
Standards 7, 33, 80, 97, 129-130, 172, 178, 195, 199-200, 205-206, 208
State
 Associations 66-67, 155, 157, 159, 161, 163, 165
 Department of Education 5, 54, 59, 125, 146, 148, 151
 Directors of
  Gifted Education 143, 145, 147, 149-151, 153
 Programs 11
 House Indianapolis 147
 Initiatives 0-1, 3-5, 7, 9, 11
Status 14, 51, 65, 95, 125
Statutes 126
Statutorily 19, 34

Index

Stephens 6, 11, 55, 57
Strategy 56, 174, 182-184, 189
Strengths 55, 76, 190, 197-198
Stress 179, 183, 196
Structure 13, 72, 183, 190
Sue 32, 51-53, 89
Sued 23, 32, 46, 54-55, 85, 87, 94, 124
Suing 25
Suits 28, 34
Superior Court of New Jersey 93
Support Consortium 195
Supporting Emotional Needs 168
Supreme Court 16, 23-24, 27, 30-31, 33, 48-49, 53, 91, 95, 122
Survey 5, 69, 124-125
Surveys 134
Swanson 122-123, 128, 141

T

Table Of Cases 139, 141
Talented
  Arkansas Department of Education 144
  Children 1-3, 7-8, 11, 25, 29-30, 89, 126, 129, 133-134, 137, 169, 178-179, 185, 191, 209

Talented *(continued)*
  Education
  Colorado Department of Education 144
  District of Columbia Public Schools 145
  Illinois State Board of Education 146
  Iowa Department of Education 147
  Kansas State Board of Education 147
  Kentucky Department of Education Division of Professional Development 147
  Maine Department of Education 148
  Maryland State Department of Education 148
  Nevada Department of Education 150
  Office of Special Education
  Alaska Department of Education 143
  Oklahoma Department of Education 152
  Ouachita Baptist University 157
  Report 5, 11
  Texas Education Agency 154
  Unit Indiana Department of Education 147
  Utah State Office of Education 154
  Vermont Department of Education 154
  Washington Office of Public Instruction 155
  Wisconsin Department of Public Instruction 155

Talented *(continued)*
  Wyoming Department of Education 156
  Program Louisiana Department of Education 148
Programs
  Connecticut Department of Education 145
  Delaware Department of Public Instruction 145
  Mississippi Department of Education 149
  Oregon Department of Education 152
  Rhode Island Department of Education 153
  Tennessee Department of Education 154
Students
  Louisiana State University 160
  Position Statement 180, 189, 191
  The University of Connecticut 168
Taylor County School District 55
Teachers of Gifted 7, 49, 51-52, 63, 163, 180-181, 194
Technicalities 26
Technology 16, 126, 153
Tennessee
  Association 163
  Court of Appeals 91, 101
  Gifted 154
Term 2-3, 32, 93
Terms 6, 13, 64, 79, 92, 132, 137

Testified 89, 98
Testimony 96, 98, 102
Testing 9, 74, 76, 121, 197-198
Tests 31, 76, 97, 196-199
Texas
  Association 164
  Court of Appeals 20
  Gifted 154
The American University 85
The College Student Affairs Journal 211
The Punxsutawney Area School District 44
Theories 85-87, 205, 207
Theory 49, 56, 97, 202
Therapy 73, 85
Transfer 21, 36, 48, 51
Transportation 9, 45-47, 50, 74-75, 78, 84
Tuition 42, 45-47, 56, 74-75, 77, 91-96, 104
Tutoring 133
Tutors 39, 42, 47, 90

U

U. S. C. 11, 32-33, 39, 132
U. S.
  code 21
  Commission of Education 11
  Congress 1-3, 11

U.S. *(continued)*
  Constitutions 25
  Department of Education
    Office 11, 116-120
  Government Printing Office
    11
  House of Representatives 1
  Senate 1
Umstot, Ann 91
Uncertified 55
Underachieve 195
Underachieving 202
Undergraduate 94, 96, 194
Underserved 114, 198, 202
United
  Nations Plaza 120
  States
    code 21
    Constitution 15, 30
    Constitutions 21
    Supreme Court 30-31, 33
University of
  Arizona 101
  Chicago 96
  Illinois 209-210
  Missouri 210
  Nebraska 98
Upholding 91, 124
Using Tests To Identify Gifted
  Students 196-197
Utah
  Association 164
  gifted 154, 164

V

Vassar 96
Vermont
  gifted 116, 154, 164
  Network 164
Violations 38-39
Virginia
  Association 164-165
  programs 155
Vocational 78, 97, 110

W

Washington
  Association 164-165
  gifted 155
Waterford Jackson 161
Wechsler Intelligence Scale 76
Weiss 127
Welfare 92, 125
West Virginia
  Board of Education V.
    Hechler 27, 44, 141
  Constitution 27
  Court of Appeals 55
  Gifted Education Association
    165
  Office of Special Education
    155
  Supreme Court 27
Wichita Collegiate 41
Wisconsin
  Association 165
  gifted 155

Witnesses 22, 72, 95
Workshops 67, 157
World Council 169
Wright 20-21, 29-30, 44, 141
Wyoming Gifted 156

Y

Youngquist 98-99, 108, 141
Youth 2-3, 7, 16, 65, 68, 83, 85, 87, 89, 91, 93, 95, 97, 99, 101, 103, 105, 107, 134

Z

Zotos 51-52, 56, 58, 141